BREAKFAST CLUB

A CELEBRATION OF THE UK'S BEST BREAKFAST SPOTS AND THEIR SIGNATURE DISHES

BREAKFAST CLUB

First edition printed in 2022 in the UK

ISBN: 978-1-910863-98-5

Written by: Katie Fisher, Lizzie Morton & Megan Georgia

Photography by: Simon Burt, Timm Cleasby, Paul Gregory, Clair Irwin, Jake Morley & Carl Sukonik

Designed by: Phil Turner & Paul Cocker

Sales & PR: Emma Toogood & Lizzy Capps

Contributors: Ashley Birch, Lis Ellis, Joseph Food, Radha Joshi & Ekta Rajagopalan

me:ze PUBLISHING

Published by Meze Publishing Limited
Unit 1b, 2 Kelham Square
Kelham Riverside
Sheffield S3 8SD
Web: www.mezepublishing.co.uk
Telephone: 0114 275 7709
Email: info@mezepublishing.co.uk

Printed in Great Britain by Bell and Bain Ltd, Glasgow

WELCOME TO THE CLUB

Who doesn't love a lazy breakfast at home or weekend brunches with friends? This book is a celebration of all the best ways to start your day and more importantly, of the brilliant foodie businesses who help that happen all over the country.

We've searched out cosy cafés, chic restaurants, brunch bars, food trucks and even a repurposed double decker bus to showcase their culinary talents in our Breakfast Club. Aside from serving up the best breakfasts in town, each of these brilliant independent businesses has generously shared a recipe for one of their banging brunch dishes to make at home. We've also told their story, what makes them tick and why they're so damn good at breakfast and brunch.

From frittata to French toast and everything in between, this book takes you on a journey not just around the UK but to Australia, India, Spain, France, the Middle East and the Mediterranean. Whether you're in the mood for an indulgent plateful or a little something on toast, Breakfast Club has got you covered.

It's been an absolute pleasure bringing this book together and we hope you enjoy reading and cooking from it as much as we enjoyed creating such an eclectic collection of recipes and stories. Though it can often end up rushed or even overlooked entirely, the world of breakfast food is full of flavour and endlessly diverse, so get out there or into your kitchen and start every day sunny side up.

Enjoy!

TEAM MEZE X

CONTENTS

The Perfect Punjabi Breakfast

By bringing a little taste of home to the brunchers of Sheffield, 5Tara introduces a whole new world of flavour to breakfast.

In 2018, founder Amanpreet Singh Bawa decided to step forward and keep his culture's cuisine alive. With years of professional experience in hospitality and marketing under his belt, the biggest hurdle Amanpreet had to overcome was the Anglicisation of his culture's signature dishes. The traditional Indian flavours he grew up with were no longer connected to his roots, something he made it his mission to address.

With the help of his partner Shivangi, the pair began by opening a home takeaway service which served as the stepping stone to the 5Tara we see today. Starting by sowing the seeds to cultivate demand for north Indian cuisine in Sheffield, it's taken a huge amount of hard work and collaboration with the community to build the business to what it is today.

Inspired by Sikhism and the devotion to ensuring that nobody goes to sleep hungry, the team have echoed their roots in every aspect of the restaurant, from the name to the food to the decor. By maintaining an atmosphere that is comfortable yet traditional, 5Tara is the perfect place for a Desi Sunday Brunch. Diners can now experience authentic Indian delicacies like 5Tara's chole bhatura with tandoori pyaz or their special aloo kachore chaat, with plenty of vegan and vegetarian options to cater to everyone's breakfast cravings.

With an à la carte menu that changes biannually and a breakfast menu that changes every Sunday, there's always something fresh to try. Drawing on Shivangi's mother's cooking and the pair's shared heritage, every dish is a true reflection of the best of Indian food. With customers coming from all over the north-west for their extensive vegan menu (which accounts for over 90% of what's on offer), 5Tara attributes their success to having found just the right balance for breakfast.

5Tara has also found huge success by endorsing their doggy-friendly approach, even going so far as to create a four-course doggy menu for your furry friends! Taking their dedication to preserving their culture one step further, the team at 5Tara also support Sum Up, a progressive campaign that buys clothing from artists in India at three times the cost to make. You can show your support by taking a look in their Sum Up corner in their venue on Duke Street next time you pop in for Sunday brunch!

नमस्ते
SHEFFIELD
INDIAN TRADITIONAL & CULTURAL CUISINE
ENJOY AUTHENTIC DESI INDIAN CHAATS,
CURRIES, LASSI's, BURGERS, SANDWICHES &
MUCH MORE FROM THE STREETS OF OLD DELHI
BOMBAY & PUNJAB!
TUESDAY-SATURDAY
grab

5तारा
#SHEFFIELD

Anand
Jaimin
BOMBAY PURI
Jaimin
THIN SEV
Jaimin

SHEFFIELD
5
tara
Relish our traditional flavours

आपका स्वागत है
5
tara

Chole Bhatura

Preparation time: 30 minutes, plus overnight soaking | Cooking time: 40 minutes | Serves 2

A piece of hot and puffed-up bhatura, tangy and spicy chickpea curry with salad, all topped off with pickle on the side: what more could you ask for? Loved by many north Indians, this delicacy has Punjabi origins and thus, you can imagine the taste of this superb dish!

440g dried chickpeas
Salt, to taste
2 teabags
½ tsp cumin seeds
1 onion, sliced
2 large cloves of garlic, minced
½ tbsp minced ginger
1½ tbsp onion paste
2 tbsp tomato purée
½ tsp ground turmeric
½ tsp red chilli powder
½ tsp ground coriander
1 tsp chana masala powder
½ tsp garam masala powder

For the dough

70g plain flour
2 large tbsp wheat flour
3 tbsp semolina
4-5 tbsp refined oil, as required
Salt, to taste
1½ tsp yoghurt (curd)

For garnishing

1 tbsp chopped coriander leaves

To prepare the chole, soak the chickpeas in water for 6-8 hours or overnight.

Put a pressure cooker on a high flame and add in the soaked chickpeas along with the salt and teabags (you can also use 4-5 tea leaves wrapped in a cloth). Cook the chickpeas for 15-20 minutes. The tea will change the colour of the gravy from dark brown to black.

Meanwhile, put a pan over a medium flame with a little oil, the cumin seeds and sliced onion. Sauté the onion until golden brown, then add the minced garlic, ginger, and onion paste. Sauté the ingredients for a few seconds until the raw smell of garlic goes away and then add the tomato purée. Once the oil has separated, add the turmeric, red chilli powder, ground coriander and chana masala. Cook the tomato-onion mixture for another 2 minutes, and then add the cooked chickpeas (chole) and garam masala with a little water. Stir well to combine the masala and the chole. Check the saltiness and adjust accordingly, then allow it to cook for a few minutes. The chole is done! You can garnish with chopped onion and fresh coriander leaves.

Now for making the bhaturas. Combine the plain flour (maida), wheat flour (atta) and semolina (sooji) in a dough kneading plate, then add the oil and salt. Mix well, then add the yoghurt and knead the dough well. You can add a little water and carry on kneading. When it's done, cover with a kitchen towel and allow to rise.

Put a karahi (or a pan deep enough for frying) over a high flame. Halve the dough equally and roll both out into large puris (bhatura). When the oil is hot enough, carefully add the bhatura to the oil and deep fry. Repeat with the other half of the dough.

Plate up your chole bhatura and serve hot!

Tips from our chef: To make the bhatura soft and delicious you can add some ghee. You can add some amchur powder to the chole, to give it a spicy-tangy touch. To make the dish more enticing you can dry-roast the spices and then add them to the dish. Add a bit of soda to give a nice texture to the bhatura. To make them puff up perfectly, make sure that the oil is super-hot.

The Beauty of Brunching

Born from the life experiences and shared culinary passions of mother and daughter duo, Jane and Alexa, Aesthete offers the people of Sheffield a taste of culinary delights from around the world..

After spending thirty-two years in Greece, Jane Baxter returned to her birthplace of Walkley in Sheffield, with her daughter, Alexa Exarcopoulos. The pair wanted to create something meaningful from their experiences so, in 2019, they opened their first restaurant – Aesthete – just two blocks away from where Jane was born.

An Aesthete (pronounced es-theet) is one who has an unusually high sensitivity to beauty in art and nature. Jane and Alexa made sure to incorporate this when it came to designing the restaurant, so the interior promotes natural sunlight with large windows, an open space and a relaxing ambience. A cabin house that overlooks the Walkley greens was added in the garden area for that log cabin experience in the winter, and a garden shed outdoorsy vibe in the summer. The venue promotes an ethos that brunch isn't just about coffee and food, but also about the ambience, the presentation, the service, the nutritional value of the dishes, respecting dietary requirements, surprising taste buds, and giving exposure to uncharted recipes.

With a strong mother and daughter bond, Jane and Alexa enjoy spending any free time they have travelling the world. On these regular travels, their main aim is always to experience as much as possible from each culture they visit, especially when it comes to food. This then comes together when they create the menu for Aesthete. You will find dishes inspired by many parts of the world, from an American Pancake Stack all the way to a Persian style breakfast bowl. The team pride themselves on their homemade dishes, and the staples they offer which are all cooked from scratch such as the tomato sugo included in the Breakfast Stack recipe.

Catering for such worldly tastes means that Aesthete has unique demands of its staff because the food and service provided isn't typically part of their past experiences. Everyone on the team rises to the occasion though, and both Jane and Alexa are incredibly proud that they have adapted and overcome. Thanks to the support of Walkley's community, Aesthete has been a huge success. And with news that they've also recently opened a new venue in Crosspool, it's clear the Aesthete name is going from strength to strength.

Bailey's tiffin

Aesthete
COFFEE & KITCHEN

Kew

Breakfast Stack

Preparation time: 15 minutes | Cooking time: 30 minutes | Serves 2

This is the most popular signature dish at Aesthete. It is the ultimate combination of all the food groups, culminating in a dish of different flavours and unique textures, and providing a satisfying and nutritiously balanced breakfast or brunch.

For the tomato sugo

2 tbsp olive oil

1 onion, finely chopped

1 clove of garlic, crushed

400g tinned chopped plum tomatoes

1 tbsp finely chopped fresh basil

For the stack

5 tbsp olive oil

1 potato, chopped into 1cm cubes

Pinch of ground turmeric

½ tsp paprika

½ leek, finely sliced (or a whole one if you love leeks)

1 handful of chestnut mushrooms, finely sliced

2 handfuls of baby leaf spinach

4 slices of halloumi or bacon (or both if you're feeling extra peckish)

2 slices of bread (we use sourdough)

1 tbsp white wine vinegar

4 fresh eggs

2 tsp za'atar or dukkha

For the tomato sugo

Heat the olive oil in a saucepan, then add the onion and garlic to cook on a low heat for 10 minutes, stirring frequently. Add the tinned tomatoes and basil, as well as salt and pepper to taste. Simmer on a low heat for 15 minutes.

For the stack

Meanwhile, heat 2 tablespoons of the olive oil in a frying pan and then add the chopped potato, turmeric, paprika, and salt and pepper to taste. Cook on a high heat. Once sizzling, turn the heat down to medium and keep tossing the potatoes every now and then to ensure they are cooked evenly.

In a separate pan, cook the sliced leek in a tablespoon of oil for one minute. Add the sliced mushrooms, cook for one more minute and then add the spinach. Turn the heat down to low and stir frequently for a couple more minutes.

In yet another separate pan, heat the remaining olive oil (2 tablespoons) and shallow fry the halloumi until golden brown, or the bacon until it's cooked to your preference. Meanwhile, toast your bread and butter the slices if you wish.

Bring a pan of water to a boil, add the white wine vinegar, individually crack your eggs into a cup and carefully pour them into the boiling water. Poach the eggs for approximately 2 minutes 30 seconds. Using a slotted spoon, take the eggs out of the water and place on some kitchen roll to absorb the excess water.

To serve

Grab two plates and use the toast as a base, topped with the sautéed potatoes and the braised leek mixture. Carefully place your poached eggs on top, spoon the sugo over each egg, and sprinkle with za'atar or dukkha. Enjoy!

Meals on the Bus

Operating out of a 1980s Bristol VR Double Decker,
The Bus Café does exactly what it says on the tin!

In December 2015 new neighbours Simon, Jodie, Lois and Xander discovered their shared dream of opening a café over pints at the local. In the face of high rents and little spare cash, an idea came to them about buying and converting a bus... and in March 2016 that bus was delivered! They parked 'Rosie' in a popular junk-yard shopping destination and converted her into a restaurant complete with kitchen, recycling and re-using wherever they could, and The Bus Café opened for service in May 2016.

Based on the seafront of Margate Mains Sands, uninterrupted sea views are just one of the many things that attracts customers from far and wide to The Bus Café. Their approach to breakfast is quirky and playful; their most popular offering is an inventive spin on the Full English, best known to their customers as The Hangover, which came third in the 'UK Breakfast of the Year 2019' before going on to win it the year after. And that's not the only award under their belt; they also held top spot for the South England Prestige Awards in both 2020 and 2021.

The team are conscious of catering to everyone's needs when it comes to their menus; everything is cooked with dairy-free ingredients, in a nut-free kitchen and, aside from the organic sourdough, all their food is gluten-free. With their South African background, Xander and Lois bring a Braai element to the lunches, and Jodie and Simon have always been massive breakfast fiends! Suppliers also play a large role and wherever they can, the team make sure to source locally: Garage Coffee, Woodlands Farm, Nash Farm, Butchers of Brogdale, D.W.G. Meats of Cliftonville and Grain & Hearth to name just a few.

When searching for a new location, the team tracked down the owner of what was a formerly derelict site and turned it into a popular street food destination on Margate's seafront. There are now five vendors including their coffee supplier Garage Coffee, Po'Boy (The Creole Fish Hut) and Pork & Co, plus a cocktail bar which they also own and manage. Along with The Sun Deck where The Bus Café resides, you can also find their food at Cliffs, a café/record shop and Stirling Hair Salon in Cliftonville across town.

There are even more exciting times ahead for The Bus Café thanks to a potential collaboration offering amazing barbecues on summer evenings, so next time you're in Margate make sure you get off at this stop!

Tips
D DRIVERS SEAT
USED TICKETS
PLEASE MIND THE STEPS

PUSH ONCE
3

BREAKFAST MENU.
BIG BITES.
THE HANGOVER National Breakfast of the year award 2019
11.5
11.5

Bus Café

The Posh Breakfast

Preparation time: 1 hour, plus pickling time | Cooking time: 15-20 minutes | Serves 2

We won National Breakfast of the Year in 2020 with this dish. We've taken some classic breakfast ingredients and tweaked them with our own homemade twists, so it's entirely gluten-free and one of our most popular dishes, being just that little bit healthier (and posher) than a traditional fry up!

For the pickled beetroot

1 beetroot, peeled and grated

100ml white wine or cider vinegar

100ml water & 1½ tbsp sugar

For the pea mayo

250g frozen garden peas or petit pois

1 heaped tbsp good quality mayonnaise

For the horseradish cream

2 heaped tsp jarred horseradish

2 heaped tbsp good quality crème fraiche

For the potato rosti

2 large white potatoes, grated

½ small white onion, finely diced

Gluten-free flour, as needed

For the mumbled eggs

Vegan spread or butter

2 free-range eggs

To serve

Fresh greens

Good quality smoked salmon

First, prepare the pickled beetroot. This ideally needs to be done at least an hour in advance but is better if done the day before. In a saucepan, bring the vinegar, water and sugar to the boil, season with salt and pepper, then once dissolved leave to cool for a few minutes.

Meanwhile, place the grated beetroot into a large glass jar with a lid. Pour the slightly cooled pickling liquid into the jar, fully covering the beetroot. Set aside for at least an hour (ideally overnight).

Prepare the pea mayo by blanching or steaming the garden peas or petit pois until tender. Drain and blitz them with a hand blender until the texture represents a rough mashed potato. Mix the mayonnaise into the peas to create a lovely light green mash. Next, mix the horseradish into the crème fraiche, adjusting the strength to suit your own taste. Rinse the grated potato in clean cold water for a few minutes to release the starch, then drain thoroughly. Using a tea towel or piece of muslin, squeeze out as much liquid as possible, then transfer the potato to a dry bowl and add the diced onion. Add a few spoonfuls of flour and mix by hand. When the mixture starts to hold its form, it's ready to cook.

Using burger rings if you have them, form the rosti on a clean chopping board and compress by hand. Add a few tablespoons of cooking oil to a non-stick frying pan and get it pretty hot. Transfer the rosti to the pan, move them slightly so they don't stick, then keep turning while cooking to a lovely even golden colour. The outside should be nice and crispy with the inside fluffy and fully cooked through. This takes about 10-15 minutes. Meanwhile, warm some vegan spread or butter in another non-stick frying pan. Crack the egg into the pan, ensuring the yolks stay whole. Carefully scramble the whites, keeping the egg together like a fried egg. Once the whites are cooked, season with salt and pepper.

To serve

Add a few fresh green leaves to the plate (we use baby spinach and spicy rocket), place the potato rosti in the centre and spread a large dollop of pea mayo over the rosti. Transfer the mumbled egg onto the pea mayo, add a nice big portion of smoked salmon on top (cut into 20mm ribbons), then a tablespoon of pickled beetroot and a dollop of horseradish cream. Grind over some black pepper to finish.

Breakfast From the Land Down Under

Friendly and fun-loving Café Mangos has made the most of an unusual and compact space to produce deliciously fresh food, which is also served at their sister venue in Sidmouth.

A chance encounter led Fay to become the owner of Café Mangos in Exeter at the age of just 20. She had flown back from Sydney, where she was living and managing a bistro, for her mum's birthday and bumped into her former employer who mentioned that the café was being sold. Although it needed work and presented certain challenges (the building itself is a brick cellar built in the 1800s) Fay felt she had been in the right place at the right time. A few months later – having stripped out the entire place with her dad, handily a construction worker – she reopened with the same name but a brand new look in March 2016.

Inspired by the café's beautiful setting on the quayside of the River Exe, Fay has introduced a dose of Australian hospitality to Devon with her focus on breakfast and brunch. The menu was designed to create a relaxed environment where people can bring their kids, their dogs, or come alone at any time of day. It's also based around the small storage and kitchen space the chefs work within, which their skill and Fay's vision have turned into a huge advantage, meaning they take deliveries of fresh produce every morning which all has to be prepared and served that day. Everything is grilled or baked (no deep frying as extraction fans aren't allowed!) and there's no fuss, just quality ingredients.

During the summer, Café Mangos also opens on Thursday to Saturday evenings when nibbles and cocktails are available alongside the wine and beer menu. Head over to Sidmouth and you'll find Fay's second venue, Milson's Point – another nod to where she lived in Sydney – also open from daytime to evening in the summer. This much larger premises lends itself to restaurant-style food but the 'fresh in, fresh out' ethos applies here too, from fish and seafood to meat which is now all completely traceable back to where it was raised.

Fay credits her fantastic team with making Mangos and Milson's Point what they are today; some staff have been with the original café since it first opened and all treat the business like it's their own, a rare thing that gives both venues their warm atmosphere. The next exciting development for her business is 'Mangos on the Move' – a refurbished horsebox – which will bring the same menu as its namesake to festivals and popular outdoor spots across the Southwest from May 2022, starting from Darthaven Marina in Kingswear, Dartmouth so watch this space!

MANGO'S
CAFÉ & BAR

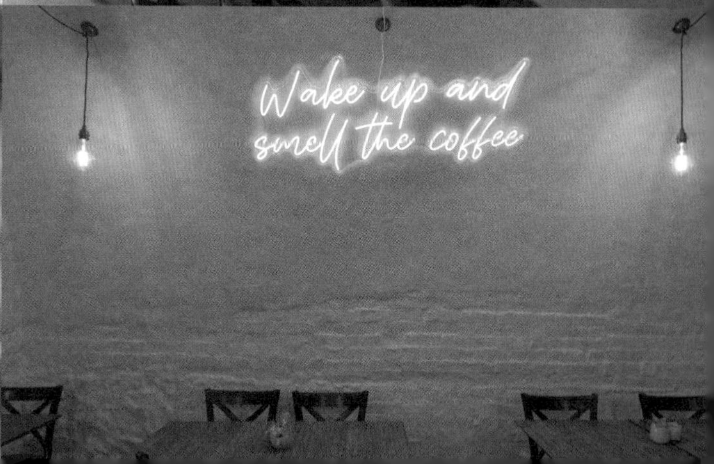
Wake up and
smell the coffee

Spicy Smashed Avocado with Poached Eggs

Preparation time: 15 minutes | Cooking time: 5 minutes | Serves 2

Smashed avocado has been our most popular dish since we opened back in 2016 and it's one of the only dishes we've left untouched on our seasonal menus. It's simple but delicious, packed with healthy fats, omega 3 and vitamins to get you through your day!

3 ripe avocados
50ml extra virgin olive oil
Salt and pepper
1 lemon
1 fresh chilli, chopped
50g cherry tomatoes
75g feta cheese
4 slices of sourdough bread
75ml white wine vinegar
2 eggs
A pinch of watercress (optional)

Before you start any cooking, fill the kettle and pop it on to boil while you prep. Halve the avocados by slicing around the stone. Remove the stone and scoop out the avocado with a spoon.

If you're making avocado for the next day or in a larger batch, you'll need to add plenty of lemon juice into the mix. Once you've put it in a storage tub, gently but firmly drop the tub onto your counter or work surface to knock out the excess air and then push a layer of cling film down onto the avocado. This will keep it from going brown!

Put the avocado into a bowl and add 25ml of the extra virgin olive oil. Season well with salt and pepper. Juice your lemon into the mix, being careful to remove any pips that may fall in. Time to smash! Using a fork, mash the avocado, making sure not to create a paste as you want it to retain some texture.

Slice off the end of the chilli and then open it lengthways, using the blunt side of the knife to remove any seeds. Cut into small slices. Cut the cherry tomatoes into quarters and cube the feta. Slice the sourdough and set aside for the moment.

Pour the hot water from the kettle into a deep saucepan, bring to a gentle boil and add the white wine vinegar. With a spoon, stir the boiling water until it makes a whirlpool. Crack your eggs into the centre of the whirlpool and leave them to cook for 2 minutes.

While the eggs are poaching, toast your sourdough. Once toasted, pour the remaining olive oil over the sourdough and begin to plate your dish!

Top your toast with the smashed avocado, cherry tomatoes, feta and chilli. Take out the eggs out of the pan and gently put them onto a clean tea towel to remove excess water, then place these on top of your avocado dish. Garnish with watercress if using and enjoy!

Sitting on the Deck of the Bay

With an incredible harbourside location and stunning venue, The Canteen is renowned for its breakfast, best enjoyed while watching the ships roll in to set you up for the day.

Lucy Branson's family had always run restaurants, and she met her future husband in a restaurant where they both worked as teenagers, so it's no surprise they were drawn back to hospitality. Luckily for the people of Portsmouth, they also chose to move back home and first took over a tearoom in Southsea. In 2015 they felt ready for another project, which turned out to need all their experience and passion as they created The Canteen from scratch in a derelict former barracks in the Hotwalls Arts Quarter.

Today, the partners in life and business have collaborated with the rest of their family to bring us The Coastal Kitchen Family, encompassing four restaurants and a wine wholesaler. Lucy emphasises how instrumental the wider team are to its success too: "The way we run our business is very much about looking after the staff first, then everything else falls into place. Our company values are family, community, hospitality and honesty which run through all our decision making, and our people are the nuts and bolts that keep everything running smoothly."

The Canteen sits on the Millennium Walkway in a popular urban area of Old Portsmouth, so it was very important for the team to find out what their customers wanted, which turned out to be great breakfasts! There's a servery filled with freshly baked pasties, sausage rolls, cakes and scones to take away as well as seating indoors under the exposed brickwork and statement light fittings, or outside on the beautiful decking with unbeatable sea views.

Changing seasonally while retaining its core classics, the menu is focused on flavour and cooked by chefs who make everything they can in-house. The Canteen Stack is an absolute bestseller – think refined Full English featuring truffled mushrooms, potato rosti, perfect poached eggs, smoked streaky bacon and hollandaise sauce – with the ham hock eggs Benedict a close second. They are also committed to offering great vegan and gluten-free options without any compromise on quality, again all made from scratch with produce from local greengrocers, butchers and bakers.

Thanks to such a unique and stunning setting, The Canteen is becoming ever more popular as an events and wedding venue for private hire too. Huge windows provide a constantly changing backdrop of sea and sky, set against the rustic and cosy interior whose minimalist feel is partly due to the listed status of the building, but also lets the beauty of the surroundings speak for themselves.

ICE CREAM
THE HUT
AT THE CANTEEN
JUDE'S ICE CREAM
TRULY CHOC
STRAWBERRY
SALTED CARAMEL
VANILLA
MINT CHOC
MANGO SORBET
1 SCOOP: £2.50
2 SCOOPS: £3.50
FLAKES: 20p

WIGHTLINK

GREAT BRITISH ICE CREAM
Jude's
ICE CREAM

Spice Island Scrambled Egg

Preparation time: 15 minutes | Cooking time: 5 minutes | Serves 2

Historically, Old Portsmouth was given the name Spice Island as the first place that spices landed from Jamaica... or, as some say, due to the "spicy side of life" demonstrated by sailors in the port. Either way, we've taken inspiration to add some punch to this breakfast time favourite.

2 tsp diced red onion
1 tsp minced garlic
1 tsp sliced green chilli
3 tsp spice mix (see below)
1 tbsp butter
6 eggs
Salt and pepper
2 tsp chopped fresh coriander
2 slices of buttered sourdough
2 tbsp Greek yoghurt
Drizzle of hot sauce
1 tsp black onion seeds
Pea shoots, to garnish

For the spice mix

6 tbsp ground turmeric
5 tbsp ground coriander
5 tbsp ground cumin
3 tbsp curry powder
2 tbsp paprika
1 tbsp chilli powder
1 tbsp garam masala

First, make the spice mix by simply combining all the ingredients. Store in an airtight container. This will make plenty to use another time.

Heat some oil in a pan and add the onion, garlic and chilli. Sweat on a low heat for a few minutes then add your spice mix. Stir and then add the butter.

Quickly crack the eggs into a mixing bowl and whisk, then season with salt and pepper. When the butter is foaming in the pan, add the eggs and turn down the heat. Stir gently to a soft scramble, then stir through the chopped coriander.

To serve

Serve your spiced scrambled egg with the toasted and buttered sourdough with Greek yoghurt and a drizzle of hot sauce on top. Sprinkle the yoghurt with black onion seeds and finish with a handful of pea shoots.

A Continental Way to Start Your Day

Inspired by the flavours of Italy and France but made in sunny Manchester, Caramello of Didsbury introduced a lovely new dining perspective to the city when it launched in the summer of 2016.

The team at Caramello believe that food is a great way to meet people and make friends. When people share a meal, you can be sure the discussions about food, restaurants and recipes are going to be endless. We couldn't agree more. Upon arrival to the café, you will be greeted by a large Alice in Wonderland-esque mural on the side of the building, done by a local street artist from Manchester. Not just a pretty picture, it will really set the tone for your experience. Inside it's bright, warm, friendly, and very welcoming; with flower walls, distressed wood, and hand drawn blackboards. Their whole aesthetic makes brunch at this picturesque little café a delightful dining experience.

At Caramello, everything from the gelato to the patisseries, from the sausages and of course to the brioche loaves, is made in house by their self-taught head chef Nafa. Nafa spent time learning his trade in Lille, France, where he was surrounded by patisseries and bistros, and to this day, he is still being inspired by them. For a small place, Caramello has a wide range of choices on the menu, offering a great balance of sweet and savoury, making it perfect for families as well.

Their brunch menu is especially popular, with the Full English Breakfast and Brioche French Toast taking the top spots. Served with both fresh berries and raspberry coulis, or smothered in Lotus Biscuit and Biscoff sauce, the Brioche French Toast really is the one to try. The recipe is even included in this book, so you can give it a go for yourselves from the comfort of your own home.

The Caramello team have recently taken on a new site, which will have a very similar daytime menu, but will also be offering fully halal fine dining with an à la carte menu in the evenings. Brunch isn't the only thing to get excited about here. As they say at Caramello: "pull up a chair. Take a taste. Come join us. Life is so endlessly delicious."

You had me at
Caramello

PX125

CARAMELLO

CARAMELLO

CARAMELLO
of Didsbury

Brioche French Toast

Preparation time: 45 minutes, plus 6 hours resting | Cooking time: 40 minutes | Makes 1 loaf (21.5cm x 11cm)

At Caramello of Didsbury we've become quite well known for our signature homemade brioche loaf, and now we're treating you to our recipe, perfected by our chefs over the last four years. It's certainly a process, but the rewards are worth it!

For the brioche loaf

2½ tsp instant dried yeast
60ml full-fat milk, warmed
50g caster sugar
300g plain flour
125ml lightly whisked eggs, at room temperature
1 tsp kosher or flaky salt
150g unsalted butter, softened

To serve 4

4 eggs, whisked
200ml whole milk
1 tbsp soft brown sugar
1 tsp ground cinnamon
½ tsp vanilla extract
1 tbsp vegetable oil
25g butter

For the toppings

Mascarpone
Whipped cream
Mixed berries
Maple syrup

For the brioche loaf

Mix together the yeast, warm milk, and 1 teaspoon of the sugar. Cover with cling film and leave to bloom for 15 minutes. On a low speed, combine the sieved flour, eggs, salt, and the rest of the sugar. When the yeast mixture is ready, add that too and mix until combined. Slowly add the softened butter a little at a time over a period of about 2 minutes. When the butter is almost fully combined, turn the speed of the mixer up and mix for 20 minutes. Scrape the side of the bowl occasionally. You should be left with dough that is soft, but easy to handle.

Shape the dough into a ball and put it back into the mixer bowl. Cover with cling film and put it in a warm place for 2 hours until it's doubled in size.

Punch the dough to release any air pockets and scrape onto a floured worktop. Fold the dough, outside to in, six times. Place into a deep container or roasting tin, lined with baking parchment and lightly greased. Cover with cling film again and leave to rest in the fridge for a further 1½ hours.

Spray your loaf tin, making sure all sides are well coated. Place in the dough and cover once again with cling film. This time make sure the cling film is greased on the underside as the aim is for the dough to double in size. Leave to rise in a warm place for 2-3 hours.

Now it's finally time to bake. Preheat oven to 200°c (or 180°c fan). Remove the cling film and lightly brush the loaf with a little whisked egg. Bake it for 15 minutes until the crust of the brioche is a deep golden colour, then cover loosely with tin foil and bake for a further 20 minutes. Turn the brioche onto a cooling rack, and hey presto, you're done!

To serve

Whisk the eggs, milk, sugar, cinnamon and vanilla together in a bowl. Cut the cooled brioche loaf into 1 inch thick slices and soak them in the egg mixture, pressing the brioche so it soaks up as much of the mixture as possible. Heat the oil and butter together in a frying pan, then fry the brioche slices on a low heat for a few minutes on both sides.

Serve with a scoop of mascarpone cheese, whipped cream, berries, and a drizzle of maple syrup. Bon appetit!

Travelling Through Time

Tucked away off the beaten track in Liverpool's up-and-coming Wolstenholme area, Clockworks offers a unique take on classic British comfort food in a stylised setting that reflects the venue's industrial history.

Clockworks' story began with business partners Jordan and Calum securing a lease on a 300-year-old building in Wolstenholme Square, Liverpool. The space was almost derelict and needed a lot of work, so the owners spent a year on renovations to bring their vision and the building to life. Informed by their roots in Glasgow and hospitality experience in their adopted city, Jordan and Calum created a steampunk-themed restaurant with food, drinks, décor and even music carefully curated to reflect the merging of past and future in their venue.

The restaurant offers an experimental take on British classics, described as 'comfort food with exciting twists' which of course includes a very popular full fry up. Known for its breakfasts, Clockworks stands out of the crowd by cooking absolutely everything to order so your sausages and bacon will never be sat around or reheated. This ethos extends to their produce which is delivered weekly or even daily – there's a deliberate lack of freezers in the restaurant kitchen! – to ensure ingredients are as fresh as possible. Not only do customers benefit from top class cooking, the chefs enjoy putting dishes together from scratch and making sure every plateful is done properly.

Their approach to breakfast has proved so popular that Clockworks now serves it until 4pm, with brunch and lunch options (including sharing boards and a varied choice of small or large plates) starting from 12pm. It's not only the food that keeps people coming back though, as the classic rock and roll played loud and proud is a huge part of the atmosphere here. Music is unashamedly front and centre, even when it comes to the décor which features scrap art guitars on the walls, tying the whole vibe together alongside hearty food and industrial aesthetics.

Sometimes flying under the radar even for locals, who are yet to stumble across the historic square and former blacksmiths building, Clockworks continues to offer surprises five years down the line from its opening in 2017. Jordan is excited to lean into the love their existing customers have for the soundtrack to Clockworks, aiming to incorporate more live music into their events calendar. The breakfast won't be going anywhere though, and for a whistle stop tour through Liverpool's industrial history and Britain's much-loved culinary classics, there's nowhere quite like Clockworks.

CLOCKWORKS

CLOCKWORKS

Miners' Potato Hash

Preparation time: 10 minutes | Cooking time: 25 minutes | Serves 1-2

We are all about comfort food at Clockworks and there's nothing more comforting than potato hash. Whether for breakfast, lunch or dinner, throwing your favourite protein in with some crispy potatoes is always a winner. This breakfast version was designed to set up any worker for the hardest of jobs, even if it was a day down the mines.

1 white potato, unpeeled

3 tbsp salted butter

1 white onion, finely diced

Salt and freshly ground black pepper

Bacon lardons, cooked to your preference

1 slice of cooked Stornoway black pudding

1 cooked sausage, sliced into chunks

25g cheddar cheese, grated

½ tsp Dijon mustard

1 large egg

Dice the potato into 1cm cubes and boil for 5-10 minutes until slightly tender. Set aside to drain and steam dry.

In a medium skillet, melt 2 tablespoons of the butter over a medium heat. Add the onion, then sweat until soft.

Add the diced potatoes to the veggies and cook until golden brown. Season with salt and pepper to taste, then stir in all the cooked protein, using a spatula to chop everything together.

Combine the hash thoroughly with the grated cheese and Dijon mustard, then cook on a medium to high heat and refrain from flipping to crisp up the base.

In a separate pan, melt the remaining tablespoon of butter over a medium heat and crack in the egg. Cook until the whites have set, which should take 3-4 minutes.

Serve up the hash with a fried egg on top of each portion.

All It's Cracked Up To Be

Nestled in its own jungle of greenery, The Crafty Egg is a rising star in the heart of Bristol. It's no wonder this small café has evolved into the number one brunch spot!

Starting as a real estate agent with a love of scotch eggs, Ben founded The Crafty Egg to showcase some of the delicious recipes found on his travels. Opening their doors in 2016, the team wasted no time in establishing a name for themselves, attracting huge queues of eager customers with lines often trailing down the road.

The modest interior is deceiving, being home to dozens of indoor plants and an extensive menu of inventive brunch dishes (including vegan and vegetarian options). The cosy seating encourages a homely ambiance and laid-back vibe which draws customers back time and time again. Ben also extended his culinary ingenuity to the décor, upcycling Extract coffee bags into lampshades which add a rustic touch to the beautifully preserved 18th century building.

In homage to their local independent businesses, the menu at The Crafty Egg features produce from nearby suppliers at Buxton Butchers and Clarence Court as well as impressive artwork from resident artists. Thanks to a fantastic team of front of house and kitchen staff, the venue has amassed an ever-expanding customer base while continuously refining their menu to cater to everyone. Everything from crowd pleasers like poached eggs to homemade kimchi (for the more adventurous) is served on sourdough toast, still warm from Orchard Bakery. "The bread delivery is my favourite part of the day, the trail of flour left by our friends at the bakery and the comforting smell of fresh dough wafting through the café," manager Holly shared, a heart-warming insight into how the team at The Crafty Egg operates alongside local suppliers.

The team's success has landed The Crafty Egg the number one spot on TripAdvisor's brunch venues in Bristol as well as the 14th best restaurant in Bristol with aims to crack the Top 10 in the near future. Taking advantage of the lockdown, Ben has honed in on providing excellent service to a smaller capacity of customers, curating the experience at The Crafty Egg to ensure that every individual leaves with a smile and a full belly!

The Crafty Egg continues its success in their brand new venue in Fishponds, introducing a bar and pizza nights alongside their renowned brunch menu. By continuing to craft a cosy vibe in an up-and-coming area of Bristol, The Crafty Egg has joined a larger community of independent businesses in the stunning Victorian suburb. Staying true to their roots, the team have kept it local, offering beer from Bristol Beer Factory and a range of homemade pizzas in this revitalised boozer.

VANS

CRAFTY EGG

OPEN
MONDAY
FRIDAY
SATURDAY
SUNDAY

Salmon and Potato Hash

Preparation time: 20 minutes | Cooking time: 35 minutes | Serves 4

Light, fresh and different without being complicated or pretentious, our salmon and potato hash offers an explosion of complementary flavours, with a balance of sweet and spicy from the gochujang and lime crème fraiche, adorned with a perfectly runny fried egg, surrounded by smoked salmon and decorated with sesame seeds.

3 large or 4 medium potatoes
Vegetable oil
120ml crème fraiche
1 lime, zested and juiced
500g kale
4 large eggs
180g smoked salmon
20g each sesame seeds, micro coriander & micro shiso

For the pickles

150g each water, sugar & white wine vinegar
1 tbsp coriander seeds
1 tsp cumin seeds
Pinch of smoked chipotle
2 cucumbers
20g fresh dill, finely chopped

For the gochujang chilli relish

1 shallot
2 cloves of garlic
Thumb-sized piece of fresh ginger
200ml tomato ketchup
50ml rice wine vinegar
100ml gochujang paste

Start by chopping your potatoes into 1cm cubes. Boil them in a large pan of water for 20 minutes, then drain and leave to steam dry. Meanwhile, preheat your oven to 180°c and place a well-oiled tray inside to heat up. Once the potatoes are dry, place them on the hot oiled tray and season with salt and pepper to taste. Bake in the oven for about 25 minutes or until golden brown.

While the potatoes are cooking, prepare your accompaniments. For the pickles, combine the water, sugar, vinegar, coriander seeds, cumin seeds and smoked chipotle in a saucepan over a medium heat. Meanwhile, peel or finely slice the cucumbers into ribbons and toss them with the fresh dill. Leave the pickling liquid to cool before pouring it over the cucumber and dill, adding a pinch of salt to taste, then set aside while you make the rest of the dish.

For the gochujang relish, peel and finely dice the shallot and garlic, peel and finely grate the ginger, then sweat them in a pan until softened. Add the ketchup, vinegar and gochujang, then leave to cook for 15-20 minutes, stirring occasionally.

Mix the crème fraiche with the lime zest and juice in a small bowl, then set aside in the fridge. Chop and rinse the kale, then blanch it for 1 minute in boiling water, drain and refresh in iced water.

Once everything is cooked and ready to serve, fry the eggs to your liking (we do ours with a runny yolk). They should take about 3 minutes to cook. In the meantime, place the potatoes into a large mixing bowl with 2 tablespoons of the gochujang relish and all the prepared kale, then toss the ingredients together.

To serve

Spread 2 tablespoons of lime crème fraiche onto each bowl or plate. Cover with a hearty pile of the potato hash, place a fried egg on top, add the smoked salmon and drained cucumber pickle, then garnish with the sesame seeds and micro herbs.

The Best Welsh Brecwast

With full dedication to great food and their local community, the team at Crwst have baked their way into the hearts and bellies of their customers.

From cooking with his Mamgu (grandmother) as a child to growing a successful business from the same kitchen, Osian shares his passion for baking with everyone who visits Crwst. Along with his wife, Catrin, the pair have curated a total of three venues, each one echoing their aim to deliver delicious treats in a relaxed and accessible environment in west Wales.

Famous for their homemade hash browns and pancake stacks (with or without booze), Crwst has taken Wales by storm. Since opening their flagship Cardigan site in 2018, the couple have expanded massively, now employing more than 50 dedicated staff members over three sites. With award-winning Pembrokeshire Sea Salted Caramel and Crunchy Granola, a variety of vegan and vegetarian options as well as first-class Welsh produce, the key to Crwst's success is evident in their passion for providing amazing food and fabulous service.

With seasonal menu changes every quarter, Osian and his team make full use of the fresh produce on offer. With customer favourites like French toast and pancakes, you'll always be able to find something tasty to eat, topped with the highest quality berries, homemade spreads and ice cream.

As first-language Welsh speakers, it's no surprise how dedicated the couple are to sustaining their local community, going so far as to design bespoke 'Bake-at-Home' kits to support Hiut Denim (a local company who makes jeans, but turned to making scrubs for the NHS during the first lockdown) and planting a tree for every £20 online spend. The team also launched a Crwst cookie kit, the proceeds of which have been donated in support of the crisis in Ukraine. Having been supported by local shops in the early stages of Crwst, the pair also sources their produce almost entirely locally, taking full advantage of incredible suppliers like Bay Coffee Roasters and Caws Teifi Cheese.

Despite having won Best Rural Start-Up in the UK in 2019 and Most Welcoming Café in South Wales the same year, the team have no active plans to expand just yet, deciding to focus on improving on the business as it is currently. With three sites under their belt (the café in Cardigan, their beachfront location in Poppit Sands and the independent bakery), there's space for everyone at Crwst, whether it just be for coffee or their infamous Welsh Brekkie. Head over to their website to book a table, support their causes online or see what a day in the life of a Crwst baker looks like!

CRWST
DELI · BRUNCH · DINNER · BAR

CRWST

Hanes yr Adeilad

CRWST

CRWST
Caramel
GIFT SET
PEMBROKESHIRE SEA SALTED CARAMEL

Breakfast Pancakes

Preparation time: 10 minutes, plus 30 minutes resting time | Cooking time: 15 minutes | Makes 12

This is the most sought after brunch dish at Crwst which highlights some of the tastiest and freshest local treats. By elevating the modest pancake into something even more delicious, the team at Crwst have taken brunch to a new level.

For the pancakes

338ml milk

1 egg

240g plain flour

35g baking powder

42g caster sugar

42g butter

For the toppings

250g mixed berries (or any berries of your choice)

65g caster sugar

500g natural yoghurt (we love Llaeth Y Llan)

500g granola (try Crwst's homemade granola!)

A drizzle of honey or maple syrup

To make the berry compote, place the berries and sugar in a pan on a high heat and bring to the boil. Reduce the heat to medium and let the fruit simmer for 1 minute. Take off the heat and leave to cool.

For the pancake mix, pour the milk and crack the egg into a mixing bowl. In a separate bowl, sift the flour, baking powder and sugar together. Melt the butter.

Quickly tip the dry mix into the milk mix and whisk until just combined, making sure not to over mix as this will make your pancakes tough! Add the butter and whisk until combined.

Leave the mix to stand for 30 minutes. In a non-stick pan, melt some butter on a medium-high heat. Using a ladle, spoon in the pancake mix (you can make these as big or as small as you like!) and let it cook. Flip the pancake over once one side is golden brown. Repeat this process until all your pancakes are cooked!

Now it's time to stack your pancakes. Dollop a spoonful of berry compote, yoghurt and a sprinkle of granola between each layer. Repeat this process until you get three stacks. Drizzle some of your favourite honey or maple syrup on top to finish. Devour and enjoy!

Just My Cup of Tea

Colourful café Cup in Aberdeen is much more than a breakfast pitstop – enjoy all-day brunch from a unique menu in a setting that will whisk you away for a meal to remember!

When Angela Kozak established Cup in 2013, the initial idea for the café was based around afternoon tea, which was becoming much more popular and not readily available in Aberdeen at that time. However, the focus quickly shifted as Angela realised that the same thing was true for brunch and there was a gap in the city for an all day offering. She developed the menu herself, drawing on extensive travels in Dubai, Thailand and around the UK where she always kept an eye out for something a little bit different.

Cup's food is designed to create an experience, not simply breakfast on a plate, and to stand out through the presentation and attention to detail. Avocado toast – served in multiple ways – is still one of the best sellers alongside the unique 'morning tea stand' featuring sweet and savoury tiers of breakfast nibbles such as mini bacon rolls, pancakes and pastries. The variety of breakfast boards are also really popular, showcasing the café's knack for making even everyday favourites look beautiful. Head chef Craig, who has worked with Angela for over five years, ensures that everything leaving his kitchen is immaculate and plated with pride.

The importance of aesthetics carries through to Cup's décor; everywhere you look has something different going on. The huge selection of teas on the menu is represented by a map on the wall identifying tea-producing regions, and the 'art wall' made up of flowers and pick 'n' mix sweeties captures everyone's eye. Even the toilets have an Alice in Wonderland theme! Cup is colourful, endlessly Instagrammable and somewhere to enjoy a memorable morning that's much more than a cup of tea or coffee.

Angela says that her staff are what really makes the business: "you really notice it changing when people leave, which doesn't happen too often thankfully as everyone enjoys the atmosphere here." This genuine team spirit and engagement with customers are key factors that bring people back on both sides of the café. Local suppliers are an important part of this synergy too, from The Bread Guy in Aberdeen to fruit and veg from Turriffs of Scotland.

Angela has some exciting next steps planned for her thriving business, starting with all-weather outdoor seating which will seat an extra 24 people for year-round al fresco brunching, boosting the city centre's café culture. Angela is also looking at second venue in Aberdeen, so if we're lucky there could be a Cup mark two coming soon!

CUP

HEY

GENERAL STORE
STORAGE

Mini Slider Brekkie Board

Preparation time: 3-5 minutes | Cooking time: 15-20 minutes | Serves 1

If, like me, you can never make up your mind what you want for breakfast, then this is an ideal choice. 'A little bit of everything' is how I like to think of it. It's like a breakfast buffet on one plate!

1 pork sausage

1 rasher of bacon

Selection of fruit (we use ¼ of a banana, 2 strawberries, 6 blueberries and a couple of grapes)

30g cereal or granola of your choice

Orange or apple juice

1 egg

White vinegar, for poaching

3 mini brioche rolls

Butter, for spreading

Heat your oven to 180°c. Pop your sausage and bacon in for around 15-18 minutes, until cooked all the way through. Alternatively, you can fry them instead. Put a timer on for 15 minutes to check the meat, so you know when to start poaching your egg. While the sausage and bacon are cooking you can get your other board contents ready.

First, prepare your fruit stack. Slice your banana and the strawberries, or whatever fruit you're using, and pop everything into a little jar or bowl. Next, choose the granola or cereal you want to use and pour this into a separate small bowl. If you're using granola, we recommend layering it with natural yoghurt and then topping with more fruit and honey. For cereal, just use the milk of your choice. Pour your juice of preference into a small glass.

Next, pour boiling water into a small saucepan and place over a medium heat. Adding a small amount of white vinegar to the water will help to stop the egg from splitting. The water is ready when small bubbles form on the bottom of the pan. Once the 15 minute timer ends for the sausage and bacon, check that they are cooked all the way through and, if you're happy with them, you can now add the egg to the saucepan. For a perfect poached egg, cook for 3 minutes and 30 seconds.

While the egg is cooking, open up your mini brioche rolls and spread on the butter. Now you can assemble your juice, granola or cereal and fruit bowl on the board. Once the egg is cooked, add that to one slider, the sausage (cut up to fit) to another and the bacon to the last one. Add these final elements to your brekkie board and enjoy!

Photographer to Foodie

Having spent most of his career professionally photographing lovely food and restaurants, Jake Morley decided to put himself on the other side of the camera lens.

When the pandemic hit in 2020 and Jake's photography work came to a standstill, he took the initiative and, using a converted 1960s horsebox, opened Dusty's Kitchen. Jake wasn't sure what to expect but he did know there was potential for a good coffee van in the village. He snapped up this new opportunity to explore his longstanding passion for food, in a way he'd never truly tried before. He was pleasantly surprised (and delighted) when, after only two weeks, the business was inundated with queues forming on a daily basis!

Rather than stretching themselves thin trying to offer a large number of options, Jake and his team have provided their customers with a simpler, more personal menu. You can guarantee they've poured their heart and soul into each dish, perfecting them until they're of the highest standard. Some favourites of their purely vegetarian cuisine include the Halloumi Hash which is featured in this book, a House Granola, and even some Vegan Energy Balls: chia seeds, mixed nuts, dates and coconut oil, all blended together and rolled into these healthy treats.

Almost everything is sourced locally, from the freshly baked cakes found in Jake's own village of Sully, to the coffee roasted in Cardiff, just three miles down the road from Dusty's trading spot. The Kitchen even offers their own ethically sourced vegan coca cola.

With a slightly hippy and quirky vibe, the van has accumulated a loyal following of regular customers and in the pandemic it became a real gathering point. Dusty's Kitchen even gave those who had always lived in the village without ever meeting the chance to get acquainted. As Jake says, "it's a real positive zone with a strong sense of community." Everyone on the team plays an important role in providing a safe space for people to come and enjoy the food at Dusty's. There is even an artist on the team, who has decorated the van's interior with her own work.

At Dusty's Kitchen, they're currently in the process of renovating another van which will add a mobile element to the business. There are already plans to visit events and festivals, meaning the Kitchen will soon be reaching customers on a wider scale: Dusty's on Tour, if you will. Just for a final wholesome touch, Dusty's Kitchen is actually named after Jake's dog – how lovely!

DUSTYS CAKES
CLASSICS
Welsh Cakes x2 £1.50
Lemon Drizzle £2.50
M&M Cookie £2.50
SPECIALS
Sultana Flapjack

DUSTYS

DUSTY'S
MilkShakes
Strawberry
Chocolate
Vanilla
£3

Dusty's
Hot Coffee
Fresh Food
Good Vibes

Dusty's Halloumi Hash

Preparation time: 5 minutes | Cooking time: 10 minutes | Serves 6

This is our House Special: super simple, super filling, super tasty and great anytime of the day. Easy to make in one big frying pan too! Fry your eggs to taste, but at Dusty's we like our eggs runny.

- 300g couscous
- 1 bunch of spring onions, finely chopped
- 450g (2 blocks) quality halloumi cheese, diced
- 2 x 400g tins of chickpeas, drained
- Chilli flakes, to taste
- 6 eggs
- Salt and pepper, to taste
- 1 lemon
- Freshly chopped coriander, to garnish
- Rocket leaves, to serve

Put the couscous on to soak, remembering the 1:1 rule. For 300g of grains you'll need approximately 300ml of boiling water. Stir the couscous briefly and cover.

Heat some olive oil in a frying pan over a high flame, then fry the spring onions and diced halloumi. After a few minutes, when the halloumi starts to colour, add the drained chickpeas and chilli flakes. You can also start frying the eggs alongside the hash, cooking them to each person's preference. Meanwhile, stir the couscous, then season with salt and pepper. Squeeze in the juice from the lemon and fluff the couscous with a fork.

To serve

Dish out the couscous into equal portions and then spoon a generous amount of the hash on top. Place the fried eggs onto each dish and garnish with the chopped coriander. Finally, serve with the rocket leaves. Enjoy!

Meet Me at Eat Me

Reinventing homely delights with Asian-inspired ingenuity is the recipe for success at Eat Me Café with over a decade of experience behind their amazing dishes.

At Eat Me Café, the gap between the east and west is drawn to a culinary close with amazing blends of Asian-inspired dishes and English favourites. Owners Martyn and Stephen opened the café 13 years ago in the small town of Scarborough, introducing traditionally Asian treats like Vietnamese drip coffee and Japanese ramen to the area.

Since then, it's been a rollercoaster for the couple. Determined to survive the national pandemic that saw the end of thousands of small eateries, the pair forged forwards to sustain their business and local community. Opting to make a difference in the lockdown, the team at Eat Me Café moved to their larger venue in the legendary Stephen Joseph Theatre and worked to feed over 6000 people in one of the most trying times the country has seen this century. Without the support of the community and the theatre, Eat Me Café would not be thriving the way it is today!

Maintaining their focus on good food and great service, Eat Me Café offers a plethora of brunch choices with gluten-free and veggie options available for most of their dishes. A firm favourite for nearly a decade is their EMC Big Boy Breakfast Burrito, a whole breakfast in a flour tortilla with the café's signature Asian breakfast relish. The menu has always been ahead of the curve, introducing items like Boba tea and Thai breakfasts well ahead of the mainstream eateries, putting this deceptively small café on the map for its innovative ingenuity.

The cosy speakeasy vibes combined with the cultural inclusion of 'Eat Me' stencilled in Thai on the bespoke table tops gives the café a unique edge, creating a cool corner to enjoy the tasty dishes on offer. In line with this quirkiness, the pair have plans to expand the brand to an Asian cocktail lounge in what once was a sex shop! Branching out but keeping the concept of east meets west, House of S&M will be an incredibly exciting new venture that is sure to bring Eat Me Café even more success.

Having been named nine years in a row under the Little Gem accolade in The Good Food Guide and infiltrating the Top Ten list of Eateries in Scarborough on TripAdvisor, it's safe to say that Eat Me Café is the place for a tasty breakfast that's a little bit different in the best way.

EAT ME @ THE SJT
GREAT FOOD COCKTAILS CRAFT BEER

PHONE

xoxo

Eat Me
EAT ME @ THE SJT
GREAT FOOD COCKTAILS CRAFT BEER

AT ME @ THE SJT
COCKTAILS CRAFT BEER

Dirty Hash

Preparation time: 10 minutes | Cooking time: 10 minutes | Serves 2

For slightly spicier breakfast, look no further than this quick and easy recipe. Adding a bit of heat to your morning routine, the guys at Eat Me Café have you sorted with their jalapeño and sesame seed Dirty Hash.

120g cubed sausage, chorizo or tofu (or a combo)

2 tbsp oil

2 potatoes, par boiled and cut into small cubes

1 jalapeño, seeds and ribs removed, finely diced

1 tbsp gochujang

Salt and pepper, to taste

¼ tsp garlic powder

½ tsp paprika

2 spring onions, sliced

2 eggs

To serve

Your choice of seeds (we use sesame)

Sliced avocado

In a large skillet over medium heat, add your chosen protein(s).

Drizzle with oil and cook until browned or, in the case of chorizo, cooked through.

Add the potato pieces and jalapeño and let them cook for 3 minutes, or until crispy and golden on the outside.

Add gochujang, salt, pepper, garlic powder and paprika. Stir to coat the protein with the seasoning.

Add the spring onions and transfer to a warm plate.

Fry off the eggs, making the pan as hot as you can without setting the fire alarm off. Get the eggs good and crispy round the edges but ensure that the centres are still runny.

Add these to the top of the hash and sprinkle with sesame seeds.

Fan the sliced avocado between the eggs.

Take a photo and post to your Instagram.

BAMBOO CHOPSTLCKS
PRODUCT OF CHINA

Helping You to be Happy

The dream of Ezra and Gil began in 2014, with a vision of creating a neighbourhood hangout for good food, coffee, dessert and those cupboard essentials.

In 2015, the coffee shop opened its doors in the vibrant Northern Quarter of Manchester. Serving a simple menu of consistently good quality food, Ezra and Gil is all about creating a place for people to come together, where even the solo diner will be right at home. Customers return time and time again to taste what it has to offer. Located on Hilton Street, business is fast paced, running efficiently and smoothly for the great mix of people that walk through their doors.

Starting out among a thriving community of bohemian bars, bustling restaurants, an array of independent shops, and of course lively music venues, Ezra and Gil quickly grew into its surroundings and created a welcoming, laid back ambience. With stripped back interiors, and an authentic industrial aesthetic leftover from the building's days working with cotton goods, this beautiful space makes you truly appreciate the surroundings and what it was built from. As of 2021, they now have two locations, the other being on Peter Street, in the very heart of the city. With the only difference being the venue itself – the menu and decor are exactly the same – you'll know you're in Ezra and Gil as soon as you walk through the door.

Italian head chef Daniel Mancini changes the menu every season, keeping things fresh and exciting. Having spent quite a few years as a chef in London, Dan's knowledge of food just adds to Ezra and Gil's ethics and its flair. He uses that Italian background to put his own twist on the delicious homemade food they serve. Some firm favourites from the staff include the lemon cheesecake french toast and the smashed pumpkin on farmhouse toast.

Derived from Hebrew, Ezra and Gil means 'Helper and Happiness' – a fitting name for the coffee shop that's all about the people. The staff members are a strong asset, there to make sure your visit is a memorable one. The team also work with local suppliers to make sure their produce is really special, such as the smoked salmon from Richard Hyman whose great-great-grandfather developed the recipe at his deli in New York, following his incredible survival on the Titanic. There are exciting times ahead at Ezra and Gil, with a third branch in the pipeline (location: top secret) so make sure to keep an eye out for them!

GOOD COFFEE
GOOD FOOD
GOOD PEOPLE

EZRA & GIL

YOU ARE MY SUNSHINE (V) 4.25
GRASS IS GREENER (VG) 4.25
EZRA SAYS...
TRY SOMETHING NEW!
EZRA'S AFFOGATO 3.00
BIG KIDS, LITTLE KIDS 2.25

Ezra says
It's sweet

VANILLA

Smashed Pumpkin on Toast

Preparation time: 10 minutes | Cooking time: 40 minutes | Serves 4-6

After the success of our smashed avocado on toast, we wanted to introduce a similar dish; pumpkin is a more sustainable, but still super tasty, option. We introduced the Smashed Pumpkin three years ago and it's been a success since. It's also a great vegan option if ordered without feta and eggs.

600g peeled pumpkin, chopped into small chunks
Olive oil
Sea salt and black pepper
400g hummus
200g pickled beetroot, drained
White wine vinegar
6 free-range eggs, as fresh as possible
Black sesame seeds
Sliced sourdough bread
Extra virgin olive oil
80g baby spinach, washed
180g feta cheese, crumbled
Pumpkin seeds
Pine nuts
20g fresh chives, finely chopped

For the smashed pumpkin
Preheat the oven to 210°c and line a baking tray with baking paper. Spread out the prepared pumpkin on the tray, drizzle with olive oil and liberally season with salt and pepper. Roast for 40 minutes, or until tender when speared with a fork.
When the pumpkin is done, remove it from the oven, transfer to a bowl and mash with a fork. Transfer the smashed pumpkin into a colander to remove the excess liquid.

For the beetroot hummus
In a food processor, blitz the hummus with the pickled beetroots until smooth and then adjust the seasoning to taste.

For the poached eggs
Put a deep pot of water on a medium heat and add a good splash of white wine vinegar. Bring the water to a gentle rolling boil. A hard boil will destroy the delicate egg whites, while if it isn't boiling at all, the egg whites won't cook quickly enough. Crack your eggs into the pot gently, close to the surface of the water. Cook the eggs for about 3 minutes and lift them out with a slotted spoon.

To serve
Spread 4 tablespoons of beetroot hummus across a plate and sprinkle with black sesame seeds. Place one slice of toasted sourdough in the centre and drizzle with extra virgin olive oil. Cover the toast with a few leaves of baby spinach, removing the stems beforehand. Spread 6 tablespoons of smashed pumpkin over the spinach and top with a poached egg. Finally, sprinkle with crumbled feta, pumpkin seeds, pine nuts, and fresh chives, then drizzle again with extra virgin olive oil.

Cambridge's Best Buns

Fitzbillies is an integral part of Cambridge, with a history stretching back over 100 years that has seen it survive through fire, bankruptcy and a world war...

The bakery and café was opened in 1920 by brothers Arthur and Ernest Mason, who used their demob money from the First World War to establish a bakery selling a vast range of cakes, including their ultra-sticky Chelsea buns. It grew into much more over the years, showing a resilient spirit in the face of a fire that burnt down the original location completely and not one but two instances of bankruptcy. During the second of these, a tweet by Stephen Fry lamenting the imminent loss of Cambridge's very best buns caught the attention of Alison Wright and Tim Hayward. As a marketing executive and food critic respectively, the couple were perfectly placed to save Fitzbillies and help it rise from the ashes once again.

They moved back to Cambridge – Alison's hometown – to rescue Fitzbillies on Trumpington Street, going on to open another branch five years later on Bridge Street, and move the bakery to another site. This enabled them to expand and produce absolutely everything for the breakfast and brunch menus: bread, cakes, ganache for hot chocolates, and of course the famous Chelsea buns. They even use local flour: white from Marriage's of Chelmsford and wholemeal from Swaffham Prior Mill to make their signature sourdough bread.

Each branch has its own slightly different food and drink offering, such as the brunch muffin stack, exclusive to Bridge Street, and the more traditional afternoon tea at Trumpington Street. Both are blue-tiled and brick-walled with an Art Nouveau sign on the older venue showcasing the businesses' unusual name. The origins of this are up for debate, as Fitzbillies may have derived from a local museum, or possibly its benefactor's illegitimate sons who were called Fitz and Billy!

Since rescuing all that heritage, Alison and Tim have enjoyed great success, with Fitzbillies picking up an award for customer service from Cambridge Bid in early 2022 as well as being designated the winners of 2020's World Chelsea Bun Awards. Their head baker Gill deserves plenty of credit for the latter, having worked for Fitzbillies over her entire 50-year career. Luckily, you can now enjoy this signature bake anywhere in the UK by ordering on their website. Their postal gift boxes includes Chelsea Buns and tuck boxes filled with local delights; the perfect way to treat yourself and others to a slice of Cambridge's culinary history. You can order yours from www.fitzbillies.com.

CAMBRIDGE

Fitzbillies
100
1920 - 2020
100
1920 - 2020

Fitzbillies
RASPBERRY JAM
227g

Fitzbillies

Chelsea Bun French Toast

Preparation time: 20 minutes | Cooking time: 10 minutes | Serves 4

Fitzbillies has produced its famous Chelsea buns for over 100 years. Made from our secret recipe, the gooey, sticky buns are a firm favourite for customers. This year the bun has made it on to the brunch menu for the first time. Grab some Fitzbillies buns and give this delicious brunch a go at home.

For the salted pecans

20g salted butter

100g whole pecans

5g Maldon sea salt

For the whipped Greek yoghurt

150ml double cream

½ lemon, zested and juiced

150ml Greek yoghurt

For the Chelsea buns

4 eggs

300ml whole milk

4 Chelsea buns

Rapeseed oil

To serve

Strawberries

Blueberries

Raspberries

Maple syrup

For the salted pecans

Preheat the oven to 180°c. Melt the butter in a saucepan, take off the heat and add the pecans. Place them onto a baking tray with parchment paper and bake until slightly toasted, around 4-5 minutes. Sprinkle the Maldon sea salt over the pecans, allowing it to stick to the butter. Leave to cool.

For the whipped Greek yoghurt

Lightly whip the cream to a soft peak and then add the zest and the juice of the lemon half. Fold in the Greek yoghurt, and then keep the mixture in the fridge.

For the Chelsea buns

Crack and beat the eggs in a bowl with the whole milk. Slice the Chelsea buns in half and place them into the egg mixture, ensuring they are fully coated. Heat a little rapeseed oil in a non-stick pan over a medium heat and cook the buns on both sides until they are golden brown.

To serve

Plate the Chelsea buns with the fresh berries and whipped yoghurt. Finally, crush the pecans to garnish and then drizzle over some maple syrup. Alternatively, you could serve the buns with crispy streaky bacon and lashings of syrup. Enjoy!

Note: If you wanted to have a go at making the Chelsea buns for yourself, the Fitzbillies way, use the recipe found in our very own Fitzbillies Cook Book. You can find it online or in our stores.

Fitzbillies

A Cracking Start to Your Day

Based in London but transporting diners around the world with an irresistible brunch menu, The Good Egg creates vibrant and colourful food that's worth jumping out of bed for.

The Good Egg began life as a street food venture and is now two independent all-day restaurants serving up dishes inspired by the flavours of the Middle East, with nods to the cuisine of Tel Aviv's street food stalls as well as the fare sold in the classic Jewish delis, grand old cafés and bagel bakeries of New York and Montreal. The first venue, based in Stoke Newington, opened in 2015 after a successful crowdfunder – testament to The Good Egg's popularity across London's street food markets – closely followed by the second restaurant in Soho.

The core team consists of Joel and Alex, who set up the original street food business, chef Oded who brought the Middle Eastern influence which became The Good Egg's main concept when he joined as co-founder, and chef Jooles who is now responsible for menu development across both sites. She works with different concepts and ingredients to suit the slightly different characters of each restaurant, producing new seasonal dishes four times a year to keep things fresh and exciting.

The Stoke Newington branch is known for its colourful brunch offering, complemented by a light and airy space featuring lots of bare brick and plain wood. This has created an approachable space that's popular for occasions, at weekends, with families and anyone wanting to while away the morning over a leisurely breakfast. It has also recently started to open on Friday evenings, with a menu of small and large plates drawing on the same culinary inspirations and largely vegetarian ingredients.

In Soho, The Good Egg has a more stylised feel to suit the vibrant area, reflected in the bright décor as well as the food. Although the menus for the two restaurants differ slightly, with Soho leaning more towards Middle Eastern style fast food including grilled meats, there is an untouchable section for both sites where dishes that everyone loves stay on year-round. Shakshuka, French toast with seasonal toppings, and the Iraqi aubergine pita – also known as Sabich in the Middle East – are firm favourites that just can't be replaced!

During the lockdowns of 2020-2021, The Good Egg shifted to takeaway like many other venues, but their offering was so unique and well-loved that it has become a huge part of the business going forward. Freshly baked babkas are now available to order online and enjoy at home, and Londoners near the Stoke Newington site can also enjoy The Good Egg's regular food menu delivered. The team are even considering another site for their next branch, so watch this space!

KINGLY
COURT

GOOD EGG

BABKA
SHAKSHUKA
TAHIN
PASTRAM
BAGELS
CHALLAH

GOOD EGG

STRONG
COFFEE

Potato, Feta and Dill Boureka

Preparation time: 1 hour 10 minutes | Cooking time: 18 minutes | Makes 9 bourekas

This version of the popular Middle Eastern filled parcel is made with fresh herbs and spiced potato. It makes a great addition to a mezze brunch spread or can be enjoyed straight out of the oven. It's most delicious stuffed with pickles, eggs and tahini.

- 170g red potatoes
- 60ml olive oil
- ½ tsp each ground cumin, coriander, paprika, turmeric and cayenne
- 150g white onion
- 2 cloves of garlic
- 100g feta
- 10g fresh dill
- 10g fresh parsley
- 1 roll of puff pastry
- 1 egg, beaten
- Smoked cheddar, grated
- Sea salt

Start by chopping the potatoes into small cubes and placing into a bowl. Drizzle the potatoes with 30ml of the olive oil, then coat in the spices and season with salt. Roast at 180°c for 35 minutes until golden, then leave to cool. Meanwhile, finely slice the onion and mince the garlic.

Heat the remaining olive oil in a non-stick pan, add the onion and garlic and cook on a medium heat until they start to soften and caramelise. Leave this to cool while you crumble the feta and finely chop the fresh herbs.

Mix the potatoes and onion with the feta and herbs, then taste to check the seasoning. Cut the puff pastry into 13cm by 13cm squares (this should make around 9 squares) and spoon 30g of the potato mix into the middle of each one. Brush the edges of the pastry with beaten egg, then fold into a triangle shape (corner to corner) and press down on the sides to seal.

Brush the bourekas with beaten egg and then sprinkle a tablespoon of smoked cheddar on each one. Line a flat baking tray with greaseproof paper and bake for 18 minutes at 170°c until golden brown. Serve the warm bourekas with soft or hard-boiled egg, mixed pickles, fresh picked coriander and tahini dressing.

THE GOOD EGG

It's Easy Being Green

The Green Rocket is a proudly independent and multi-award-winning café and restaurant in Bath, with vibrant vegan food that puts flavour at its core.

Phil Pearce always had a lifelong dream to set up his own café and restaurant. Growing up in the hospitality industry, it's safe to say he had the experience to back it. What started out as lending a helping hand in his parents' pub soon turned to taking on various chef jobs in his home city of Bath. His career then took him overseas to Australia and New Zealand, where he spent ten years working alongside some of the greats, including Peter Chaplin, Madonna's private chef. As they say, travel is a great teacher and learning on the job and seeing the world strongly influenced Phil's cooking, enabling him to expand his culinary repertoire to a wide range of cuisines and styles.

Then came the time for Phil to create something of his own. He wanted to move away from fine dining, so The Green Rocket was going to be somewhere people could come once a week, not once a year having saved up to afford it. The café and restaurant would serve decent meals at fair prices, from breakfast to dinner with good coffee and good wine available. With a focus on offering great meat-free breakfasts which were difficult to find, The Green Rocket planted themselves at the higher end of the middle of the many existing Bath eateries.

More than eight years on from its opening, the café and restaurant still have regulars who come several times a week, or every Sunday morning for breakfast. The team get to know faces and some people have been visiting since the very beginning. It all comes down to one simple element: tasty food. Some firm breakfast favourites include the Shakshuka with Tofu 'Eggs', Monster Veggie Brekky and the Banana and Berry Smoothie Bowl. They make their menus interesting, vibrant, fresh and above all delicious. Phil reckons that around 85% of customers at The Green Rocket aren't vegetarian or vegan, which goes a long way to proving that plant-based cuisine can be all those things no matter what lifestyle you follow.

Phil and the team pride themselves on sticking to high standards of presentation and flavour, which you can only achieve with great attention to detail. With an atmosphere that feels informal and full of laughter, and excellent service that makes everyone feel welcome, The Green Rocket is the place to be for the best vegan and vegetarian brunch in town.

Photography: Rob Wicks

Vanilla Poached Rhubarb Porridge

Preparation time: 15 minutes | Cooking time: 15-20 minutes | Serves 4

This recipe came about when we ran a competition at the café for the team to come up with a new porridge recipe, won by Jye the Aussie barista who developed this. It's very easy to make when good rhubarb is in season and a firm favourite in the Pearce household.

Handful of sunflower seeds (optional)
200g rhubarb, chopped evenly
80g white sugar or agave syrup
1 tsp vanilla paste
A little orange zest, to taste
100ml water
200g porridge oats
800ml oat milk
1 tbsp maple syrup

Preheat your oven to approximately 160°c if you are using the sunflower seeds as a garnish. Place them on a baking tray and toast in the preheated oven for about 15 to 20 minutes, until they turn a light golden colour.

Place the rhubarb in a pan with the sugar, vanilla, orange zest and water. Poach gently with a lid on until the rhubarb is soft. It will take about 10 minutes until the rhubarb is starting to soften but still has a little shape.

Meanwhile, combine the oats, milk and syrup in another saucepan. Bring to a gentle boil and cook for 5 minutes until the oats are tender, stirring regularly.

Divide the porridge between bowls and top with your poached rhubarb, then garnish with some seasonal berries, edible flowers and a scattering of toasted sunflower seeds if you like.

Photography: Rob Wicks

Take A Break From The Daily Grind

A fixture of Sheffield's industrial quarter, The Grind has been serving some of the best breakfasts around since 2012 and recently expanded to take not one, but two new venues under its wing.

Not long ago, Kelham Island was a somewhat derelict area of the Steel City but even before most of the redevelopments began, The Grind made a home and a name for itself there as a standout brunch destination. Manager George used to visit often with his family, never imagining that he would one day be responsible for maintaining the café's reputation, alongside owners Alp and Hakan who took over in May 2021.

One of the secrets behind its success is listening to what customers really want from them, George explains. Why reinvent a menu full of classic breakfast dishes when so many of them are firm favourites with visitors? From Eggs Royale to The Grind's own Full English, stopping here for breakfast or brunch offers endlessly delicious options including seasonal variations and specials for regulars (of which there are many) to try out through the year. Each week also brings a different flavour of pancakes and even if you don't have time to peruse the full menu and soak up the ambience, The Grind is the perfect pitstop for a take-out coffee and a snack on your way to work.

The Grind aims to make coming out for breakfast feel like a luxury, with a friendly welcome and upbeat vibe that encourages everyone to feel at home. "The team love working here and we try to make it a great place to be for them as well as our customers, because that creates the kind of atmosphere everyone enjoys," says George. Another integral member of that team is head chef Scott, who has worked at The Grind for more than half the time it's been open and knows the business inside out. His expertise in the kitchen gets the best out of great local produce, such as sausages and bacon from John Crawshaw's Butchers and The Grind's very own blend of coffee from Pollards, both based in Sheffield.

In 2022 the café became a fully-fledged restaurant group with the addition of The Grind mark two in Broomhill as well as Saw Grinders Union, an existing bar and restaurant also in Kelham Island. The latter will be a brilliant venue for hosting more events and its menu will focus on drinks and burgers for evening indulgences, while the original and brand new cafés continue to offer a breakfast and brunch experience that's well worth waking up for!

R / L
ESPRESSO 1·90 2 20
AMERICAN 2 0 2·50
CAPPUCCINO 2·70 3·00
LATTE 2·70 3·00
FLAT W ITE 2·80
MOCHA 3·20
MACCHIATO 2·30 2·6
MATCHA LATTE 0 3·20
CHAI LATTE 3·50
HOT CHOCOLATE 3·50
TURMERIC LATTE 3·50
YORKSHIRE TEA 2·10
LOOSE LEAF TEA 2· 0
OAT / SOYA + 0·40
DECAF AVAILABLE

The Grind Cafe
Kelham Island

The Grind Baked Eggs

Preparation time: 10 minutes | Cooking time: 5-10 minutes | Serves 1-2

A Grind classic based on the North African dish, shakshuka. This has been on the breakfast menu for the past few years and is a firm favourite with our customers.

Drizzle of oil
½ small red onion
1 red pepper
1 tbsp chipotle paste
1 tsp smoked paprika
500g baked beans
2 eggs
30g feta cheese (optional)
Fresh chives or dill, for garnish
Toast, to serve

Heat a small cast iron or ovenproof frying pan with a little oil while you finely chop the onion and dice the pepper. Fry them for 2 minutes on a high heat until soft. Preheat the oven to 180°c.

Add the chipotle paste and paprika to the pan, then add the baked beans and bring to the boil. Using the back of a tablespoon, create 2 wells in the mixture and crack your eggs into them.

Place the pan into the preheated oven and bake for 6 minutes until the eggs have cooked all the way through. Take the pan out of the oven and crumble the feta cheese (if using) on top of the baked eggs. Garnish with a sprinkle of finely chopped chives or dill and serve with plenty of toast.

Naughty but Nice

Stephen Fowler first introduced the idea of Hanky Panky to his wife Rekha twenty-eight years ago, when she sat down on table two in the restaurant where he was working.

Twenty years later, Rekha finally gave in and Hanky Panky became a reality! Having experienced the highs and lows of meals out with their two young boys, the couple wanted to offer somewhere everyone could enjoy. The restaurant's decor draws inspiration from Stephen and Rekha's sense of fun, with a light and bright interior that provides a comfortable environment, evoking the feelings of holidays and coming home. "We'll have three generations coming in together – grandparents, parents and kids – and they'll all take something different from the experience."

Stephen has fond memories of childhood holidays visiting his own grandparents in Blackpool, which inspired the different names they played around with originally. "Kiss me quick" and "naughty but nice" seemed to sum up the experience of indulging in a little pancake treat, and it was almost going to be called the 'Hanky Panky Pancakes Ukulele Emporium' in homage to Stephen's love of ukulele, but this seemed a little too wordy for the name badge!

Brunch is one of those meals that can be underrated, but at Hanky Panky their wish is to make sure that's not the case. Going out of their way to offer customers something for a variety of moods and tastes, the HP menu includes South Indian dosa, a deliciously spicy alternative breakfast. The Treasure Island (a dish for over 18s only!), The Fudgelicious and The Huff 'n' Puff Kati Roll – a bacon and black pudding number – are a few other firm favourites. When it comes to the menu, they take inspiration from everyone; staff will come in excited to share their new ideas, and when customers order interesting new combinations that work well, those win a place on the menu too.

Hanky Panky is made possible by a wonderful bunch of people: customers, staff and local suppliers to name a few. It is this amazing melange of people, flavours, music and creativity that makes HP such a fun place to be! As for many people, the lockdowns of 2020-2021 offered Stephen and Rekha the chance to reflect on the development of HP over the years, and consider more possibilities... "If the stars align there are definitely some exciting opportunities we could explore in the near future," says Stephen, "so watch this space!"

OPEN
HANKY
PANKY

HANKY
PANKY

Huff 'n' Puff Kati Roll

Preparation time: 1 hour | Cooking time: 20 minutes | Serves 4

Originating in Kolkata, this kati roll has an HP twist. Griddled egg on homemade roti, coated with fresh coriander chutney, topped with spicy fried onions and peppers and finished with sizzling bacon, chorizo and black pudding. This really is what brunch was invented for!

For the roti

130g plain flour

130g atta flour

A pinch of sugar & salt

200ml water

For the spicy peppers and onions

1 medium pepper, deseeded and sliced

1 medium onion, peeled and sliced

1 tsp each ground cumin, ground coriander & chilli powder

For the coriander chutney

100g fresh coriander, stalks and all

8 cloves of garlic, peeled

5cm fresh ginger & 2 green chillies

1 tsp salt & Sunflower oil

½ tsp mustard seeds, ½ tsp cumin seeds & 1 tbsp curry leaves

¼ tsp asafoetida powder

3 tbsp freshly squeezed lemon juice

To assemble the kati roll

Bacon, chorizo, black pudding

4 eggs

For the roti

Add the dry ingredients to a mixing bowl and slowly add the water. Mix by hand, aiming for a soft dough consistency. Divide the dough into 4 pieces and shape into balls before refrigerating for 10 minutes. Sprinkle a bit of flour on your worktop and use a rolling pin to roll each dough ball into a thin pancake shape. Lightly oil your tawa or frying pan and warm over a medium heat. Cook your roti one by one, flipping halfway through. They should puff up as you cook. Put to one side.

For the spicy peppers and onions

Fry the sliced pepper and onion gently until cooked to your liking. When nearly fully cooked, add the cumin, coriander, chilli powder and a pinch of salt.

For the coriander chutney

Put the fresh coriander, garlic, ginger, green chillies and salt into a blender. You may want to use a little water to get things going. Meanwhile, pour about a tablespoon of oil into a pan and add the mustard seeds before heating on a low flame. As the seeds start to turn silver and pop, add the cumin seeds and remove from the heat. Throw in the curry leaves and asafoetida. Quickly add this spice mix to the chutney while it's still hot – it should splutter – and mix together. Add the freshly squeezed lemon juice.

To assemble the kati roll

First, cook the bacon, chorizo and black pudding to your liking. You can decide how meaty you want the roll to be. Now for the fun bit! Crack an egg into a bowl and beat with a fork, then pour into a lightly oiled hot frying pan and immediately pop one of your homemade rotis on top. Once the egg is cooked, flip the whole thing onto a plate (eggy side up), smother with the fresh coriander chutney and add some spicy peppers and onions. Next, layer up the bacon, chorizo and black pudding then roll up to enclose the filling. Repeat to make 4 rolls. The final flourish is the addition of tamarind sauce or ketchup, whichever you prefer. Garnish the kati rolls with a sprinkle of fresh coriander leaves and present to your lucky brunch partners. Enjoy!

Home is where the Hart(ley) is

As is typical with all family farms, the kitchen becomes the hub, where people come together to seek nourishment and restoration through great food and company.

This is the ethos for Hartley Farm Shop and Kitchen – a unique, informal space serving up amazing food and drink sourced and prepared with great pride. Having spent his childhood growing up on a farm, Hartley's managing director, Tom Bowles, developed a healthy fascination with food. Watching cookery programmes and exploring food markets across the world filled him with awe. The sense of knowing and understanding where the food came from lit a spark in Tom's mind which has burned bright ever since. The challenge of seeking to restore that closeness to food, and the novelty of shopping in such places, was too irresistible as Hartley Farm sought a new direction, so in August of 2008, the farm shop and kitchen were born.

Hartley pride themselves on their varied breakfast menu, hearty portions and relaxed café environment. The Farmhouse Breakfast is incredibly popular, with top notch ingredients cooked to perfection. The homemade sausages are an absolute winner! The freshly ground coffee from Origin, Cornwall, blended with organic Ivy House Jersey milk from just down the road, is certainly a popular accompaniment too.

Elements of the menu change on a quarterly basis to reflect the seasons, with a focus on using local, seasonal ingredients where possible. This includes a limited amount of honey, extracted from hives on the farm, so be sure to snap some up while you can! Hartley also benefit from having a couple of small businesses based at the farm who supply them with fresh vegetables, salads and herbs on a daily basis, as well as freshly baked sourdough bread.

The focus is on cooking fresh, wholesome food that champions the seasons and the local farmers, growers and makers behind the ingredients. At the heart of the business there's a hardworking team of staff that have made the business into the triumph it is today, all doing their bit to ensure Hartley Farm Shop and Kitchen reaches its full potential. With 10 awards under their belt so far, it's safe to say they're all doing a phenomenal job.

With great success comes exciting opportunities for expansion, and June 2022 welcomed the arrival of Hartley's new café barn. Converted from some of the farm's horse stables, the team have tried to maintain certain elements to keep a level of authenticity, whilst also modernising the space and making it a bit cosier. A new venue means a new menu, and for Tom as well as Hartley's many visitors, more food can only mean more happiness.

Leg of Lamb
£18.00 per kg

Kubota

FARM SHOP
Fresh Produce
Gift Shop
Deli
Butchery

Pan con Tomate

Preparation time: 10-15 minutes | Cooking time: 5 minutes | Serves 2

The beauty of this dish is in its simplicity; choose the best ingredients and let the flavours speak for themselves. This is what we strive to do every day in our kitchen.

- 2 large, ripe tomatoes
- Salt and pepper
- 2 slices of slightly stale sourdough bread
- Olive or rapeseed oil
- 2 cloves of garlic
- 4 free range eggs
- Fresh herbs (thyme, oregano, basil)

Grate your tomato and then smush (yes, smush!) it into a pulp using a fork or spoon. Season with salt and pepper to taste.

Toast the sourdough bread and then drizzle with your choice of oil.

Peel the garlic clove and rub it on the bread, almost like you're grating the garlic using the bread. You can use as little or as much garlic as you like, depending on your preference.

Heat some oil in a non-stick frying pan and fry your eggs on a medium heat.

Meanwhile, cover your toast generously with the tomato pulp so that the tomatoes start to soak into the bread.

Top with your fried eggs, a drizzle of oil and roughly chopped fresh herbs.

Locally Inspired

With three venues and counting, Honey + Harvey are a well-established brand boasting fresh artisan food and a sister company that roasts their own coffee for modern brunching across Suffolk.

The flagship Honey + Harvey in Woodbridge was opened in 2011; co-founder Nick Ekins looked to bring Suffolk something different when it came to breakfast and brunch. Fresh artisan food and coffee roasted in Winchester by the brand's sister company are the cornerstones of the menu, and this same offering can be found at the second branch in Melton which opened six years later.

The pair became a trio in March 2022 with the Ipswich café adding a few extras to the menu, all in unique Honey + Harvey style. The look and feel are slightly industrial, inspired by the listed building housing the Woodbridge branch, and although each has its own little quirks, they're all part of an instantly recognisable whole.

The team overseeing the three cafés is comprised of director Jackie Ha, operations manager Rosie Robinson, office manager Michelle Wall and executive chef Aaron Skerritt. Aaron is responsible for Honey + Harvey's menu development but gets his chefs at each branch heavily involved with this. The senior managers are invited to regular tastings when new dishes are in contention to keep ahead of the game and focus on continuous improvement.

They are all keen to highlight great produce from Suffolk and neighbouring Essex, such as sausage patties from Procters of Ipswich, locally produced bacon from Cleavelys butchers and the locally made Stokes chilli jam that stars in one of their customer favourites: crushed avocado on toast with halloumi, crispy bacon and poached eggs.

"Bringing the best of Suffolk's food scene to the table is what makes us tick and it's also what makes us stand out to our customers," says Aaron. Whether it's freshly baked cakes – all made on-site – or black pudding from Fruit Pig, a small independent producer based in East Anglia, the chefs are always looking for new ingredients to inform their contemporary brunch style.

This approach to the food, coupled with the attention to detail in décor and of course their signature coffee, has brought customers back to the cafés time and again. With three successful branches already under their belts, the team behind Honey + Harvey hope to continue expanding, bringing what they do best to even more breakfast and brunch goers in Suffolk and beyond.

ONEY
EST. 2011
HARVEY

Suffolk Lobster Benedict Royale

Preparation time: 45 minutes | Cooking time: 10-15 minutes | Serves 2

We buy our lobsters from Felixstowe, James Hunt fisheries, which are local and the best quality. When buying lobster, pick one that smells sea-fresh and curls its tail back under its body when stretched. Ensure the claws are bound or you could get a very nasty nip!

For the lobster

1 whole lobster (approx. 500g)
1 banana shallot, roughly chopped
1 medium carrot, roughly chopped
3 cloves of garlic
Sprig of thyme
10 fennel seeds
10 peppercorns

For the hollandaise

150g unsalted butter
2 large free-range egg yolks
1 dessert spoon white wine vinegar
1 lemon, halved
Sea salt and black pepper

For the poached eggs

2 fresh free-range eggs
Splash of white wine vinegar

To serve

4 slices of sourdough, toasted
Handful of spinach, wilted
Fresh chives or dill
Caviar, to taste

For the lobster

The kindest way to dispatch a live lobster is to use a sturdy, sharp knife and push the tip firmly and quickly through the centre of the cross on its head, making sure the cutting side of the blade is directed towards the tail. Fill a large pan with water and fully submerge. Add the remaining ingredients, cook for about 6-7 minutes, then leave to cool naturally so it retains all the wonderful flavours. You can add a small amount of ice to speed this up or put it in your fridge for 15-20 minutes. Once cooled, pull off and crack the claws, then remove the luscious white meat. Pull off the tail and peel as if it were a large prawn.

For the hollandaise

Half-fill a pan with water and bring to a slow simmer with a mixing bowl sitting on top (but not touching the water). Meanwhile, melt the butter in a medium pan over a low heat, then take it off the heat and let the buttermilk separate. Place the egg yolks in the mixing bowl and keep the water simmering on a low heat. Start to whisk the yolks and then whisk in the vinegar. Keep whisking and slowly drizzle the melted butter in until fully incorporated. The result should be a smooth, thick sauce. Season your hollandaise carefully with fresh lemon juice, sea salt and black pepper to taste.

For the poached eggs

Bring a large pan of water to the boil, then lower the heat, so the water is just bubbling. Add some white wine vinegar. Crack your eggs into small individual cups and use a spoon to stir the water in a large, circular motion to create a whirlpool. Once it's really moving, add the eggs. The motion of the water will wrap the egg white around itself so the egg stays together as it cooks. Cook the eggs for 2½ to 3 minutes, then remove with a slotted spoon. Season with salt and pepper, then serve up immediately.

To serve

Plate the toasted sourdough with the wilted spinach, while you warm the lobster with a small knob of butter just until hot. Place on top of the spinach, add your perfect poached eggs, a good covering of hollandaise, some fresh herbs, a good spoonful of caviar and then it's ready to serve.

ADNAMS
SOUTHWOLD

A Taste of Denmark

With a focus on good food, great coffee and togetherness, this quirky café encourages you to leave all of your troubles at the door.

When Alex established Hygge in 2019, the premise was relatively simple: serve good coffee. From there, the cosy café has expanded to include a dizzying variety of cakes, milkshakes and savoury snacks which make the venue a firm favourite in Sheffield city centre.

Their second venue, Lykke, is a hidden gem on the edge of New Era Square has truly embodied its namesakes, 'The Little Book of Hygge' and 'Lykke'. Meaning comfortable and happy, the Scandi vibe is prevalent in the décor and attitude here, with a cosy industrialism and a team of friendly faces that make every visit enjoyable. Acknowledging that they may not be the most unique in product, Alex prides himself on providing a unique atmosphere that is completely removed from his corporate background.

Beginning from a love of coffee, Hygge/Lykke has become a collaborative project in both atmosphere and menu. While Hygge serves their amazing coffees in their Fitzalan Square venue, Lykke offers fresh daily specials and a plethora of brunch options, and there's something for everyone, with vegan and vegetarian options being the main focus of the menu. By taking their customers into consideration, the food is up for interpretation and everyone is catered to with easy alterations that make every dish bespoke. By featuring an open kitchen, you can see how every dish is prepared with care and dedication to good food with not a microwave or fryer in sight.

Working with suppliers who echo the ethos at Hygge/Lykke, Alex has forged fabulous relationships with local retailers who work tirelessly to ensure the quality of produce. From the milkshakes to the cronuts to the pizzas, everything is fresh and locally sourced.

When asked what makes Hygge/Lykke stand out, Alex says it's his staff that sets the business apart from the rest. Having bonded as a family through pandemics and adversity, it's no surprise that the team has become an invaluable part of the business. Alex also ensures that his team share in his every success, rewarding staff with incentives and prizes as well as the odd party!

Having only recently expanded, the business is putting down roots in Sheffield with aims to fully immerse themselves in the local community. Steadily climbing the ranks on TripAdvisor, it's clear to see that Lykke is becoming a firm favourite amongst locals and tourists alike.

PAWS
OF
LYKKE

LYKKE

Baked Eggs Two Ways

Preparation time: 5 minutes | Cooking time: 15 minutes | Serves 3-4

Pleasing both vegetarians and meat eaters can be difficult, but not for the team at Lykke. By adapting their baked eggs recipe to feature either meat or mushrooms, everyone will be pleased with this simple yet tasty breakfast.

For the ancho chilli tomato sauce

Olive oil

1 brown onion & 5 cloves of garlic

1½ tsp cayenne pepper & cumin seeds

1 dried ancho chilli

2 bay leaves & 3 whole pimento seeds

4 tins of chopped tomatoes

Pinch of salt and sugar

For the baked eggs with chorizo

4-5 tbsp ancho chilli tomato sauce

4-5 spinach leaves, 2 eggs & 5 slices of chorizo

1 slice of sourdough bread per person

Pinch of pul biber (dried red pepper flakes)

For baked eggs with mushrooms

1 tsp vegan butter

1 clove of garlic, finely chopped

6 chestnut or oyster mushrooms

4-5 tbsp ancho chilli tomato sauce

4-5 spinach leaves & 2 eggs

1 slice of sourdough bread per person

Pinch of pul biber (dried red pepper flakes)

For the ancho chilli tomato sauce

Place a pan over a medium heat and add a tablespoon of olive oil. Roughly chop the onion and finely chop the garlic before adding both to pan and sautéing until softened (about 5-6 minutes). Add the cayenne pepper, cumin seeds, ancho chilli, bay leaves and pimento, mixing until everything is combined well and becomes fragrant. Stir in the chopped tomatoes, cover with a lid and allow to simmer for 10-20 minutes, stirring occasionally. Add a pinch of sugar and salt to taste, mix well and continue to simmer for a further 20 minutes. Remove the bay leaves and then pour the sauce into a food processor. Blitz until smooth and then use straight away or refrigerate for up to 3 days.

For baked eggs with chorizo

Spread the tomato sauce across the bottom of a medium-size dish, then cover with the spinach leaves. Crack the eggs into the dish and add the chorizo before putting in the oven for 8 minutes at 190°c. After this time, toast the sourdough in the oven for an additional 2-3 minutes. Remove the bread and halve it, then check the eggs to ensure they are fully cooked. Remove the dish from the oven when done. Place the toasted sourdough onto a large plate and spoon the baked eggs on top. Add a pinch of salt and pul biber before serving.

For baked eggs with mushrooms

Melt the vegan butter in a pan over a medium heat, add the chopped garlic and stir until fragrant. Once combined, add the mushrooms, coating them in garlic butter and a drizzle of oil. Stir until the mushrooms are cooked. Spread the tomato sauce across the bottom of a medium-size dish, then cover with the spinach leaves. Crack the eggs into the dish and add the garlic mushrooms. Drizzle any remaining garlic butter on top and place in the oven for 8 minutes at 190°c. After this time, toast the sourdough in the oven for an additional 2-3 minutes. Remove the bread and halve it, then check the eggs to ensure they are fully cooked. Remove the dish from the oven when done. Place the toasted sourdough onto a large plate and spoon the baked eggs on top. Add a pinch of salt and pul biber before serving.

Lovingly Local

Whether you're craving a Full English or want to check out some of the fantastic local produce in the farm shop, La Hogue has something special on offer all year round.

Husband and wife team Chris and Jo Reeks opened La Hogue Farm Shop nearly twenty years ago after leaving their professional careers as chartered surveyors behind and selling their home to finance the new venture. The business has grown enormously over the years, particularly following the addition of the café in 2010, and is a real destination for both locals and holiday makers due to its amazing breakfasts and brunches.

With a simple yet tasty menu, Chris and Jo have curated a culinary experience that is accessible to all by building their menu from food they would like to eat. Jo says that their menu isn't fussy, meaning what you see is exactly what you get. By highlighting the beauty of home cooking rather than trying to overcomplicate things, Jo simply explains, "we use butter where butter should be used. We use double cream where double cream should be used." By baking 95% of their own cakes and desserts as well as using only the highest quality meat, La Hogue pride themselves on making food that is always a hit with customers, old and new. With meaty, veggie and kiddie options, there is something on offer for the whole family.

Earning its namesake from a late 17th century naval battle between the British and the French, La Hogue Farm features some extraordinary timbers reclaimed from the battleships, offering a nod to the area's local history. Outside, the café boasts a marquee for the winter, with the ability for it to be opened out in the summer. No matter the weather, La Hogue visitors can fully appreciate the stunning landscape. By striking a balance between homely and professional, the atmosphere at La Hogue makes it the perfect place for a family outing or a temporary workspace.

Jo attributes a lot of La Hogue's success to head chef Marie and café manager Julie, both of whom have been with the business since the very beginning. Together, they have been instrumental in providing the excellent food and outstanding service that makes La Hogue successful.

With plans to expand in the future, upgrade the kitchens and expand the range of products on offer, La Hogue aims to improve upon the foundations they have so lovingly curated for all these years. So, whether it's for the La Hogue English Breakfast in the café or to peruse the best local produce in the farm shop, make sure you pop in to see what tasty treats La Hogue has to offer.

Stokes

LA HOGUE
FARM SHOP CAFE

CHAIR

Breakfast Frittata

Preparation time: 15-20 minutes | Cooking time: 1 hour 5 minutes | Serves 6

This delicious Breakfast Frittata is always a winner when we put it on as a special in our farm café. It is quick and easy to make and is great for breakfast, brunch or lunch!

5 rashers of smoked back bacon
2 butcher's sausages
130g cheddar cheese, grated
6 cherry tomatoes, halved
5 fresh free-range eggs
300ml double cream
Salt and pepper

Line a 23cm (9 inch) loose-bottomed tin with baking parchment, leaving the edges to overhang the sides of the tin.

Cook your meat according to the instructions on the packaging and your preference (for crispier bacon, cook for a bit longer). Cut up the bacon and the sausages into bite-size pieces and arrange them in the bottom of the tin. Then, scatter the cheddar cheese over the meat and place the cherry tomato halves on top. Season with salt and pepper.

Crack the eggs into a bowl and beat. Add the double cream to the eggs and whisk together until combined. Set the oven temperature to 160°c fan. Pour the egg mixture into the tin, then place on a baking tray and put into the oven for approximately 30-35 minutes until set.

Remove the frittata from the oven and divide into 6 equal portions. We recommend serving the frittata with sautéed new potatoes, fried onions, and BBQ baked beans. Enjoy!

A Design for Life

With three branches in Sheffield – each beautifully designed to emphasise the spaces they inhabit – Marmadukes is a much-loved family business that's going from strength to strength.

In 2012, Clare and her husband took over a tiny café in a Georgian townhouse on one of Sheffield's oldest city centre streets. They built a loyal following based on not just the quality of their food but the experience they offered every customer, whether they popped in for a cup of tea and a scone or stayed for an indulgent brunch. Their own family was a big influence on this welcoming atmosphere; getting everyone round the table became the essence of what the Marmadukes brand is all about.

The second venue on Cambridge Street, a relaxed contemporary space with industrial touches, opened just a couple of months before the pandemic but proved its popularity once trading began again in summer 2021. The next branch became the "ultimate lockdown baby" for the Marmadukes team, who threw themselves into the project to reinvent a former post office and create the brunch destination of their dreams. The Sorting Office is reminiscent of Australian and New Zealand all-day restaurants where breakfast is the main event, enjoyed in a light and airy environment that showcases the on-site bakery and kitchen.

Though the menus differ and develop to suit each branch's unique appeal, what connects them all is Marmadukes' motto of 'best made'. This means that whatever they do is created from scratch, researched to the nth degree and the best it can be, from supplier relationships to new dishes and staff training. A key example of this ethos is the Wildfarmed flour used in the bakery. This is sourced from a producer committed to environmentally beneficial farming practices and results in Marmadukes' signature sourdough which is not only delicious, but more digestible and nutritious.

Bread is the cornerstone of head chef Sam's menu at the Sorting Office, complemented by seasonal produce with a focus on flavour. Firm favourites include the Marmuffin: a sausage patty (from Owen Taylor butchers, though all other meat is supplied by their local producer, Moss Valley Meats) and fried Cacklebean egg with Montgomery cheddar and greens on a house-made English muffin. For those with a sweet tooth, head pastry chef Becca ensures the counter is stuffed with inventive treats like caramel ganache brownies, Basque cheesecake and cinnamon-coated morning buns.

Having expanded so successfully, owner Clare is conscious of staying relevant and inclusive. "It's very important to me that we don't alienate anyone, and to see ourselves as a community hub rather than just a restaurant. A lot of that comes down to our staff, who are genuinely passionate about what we do and become part of the extended family here."

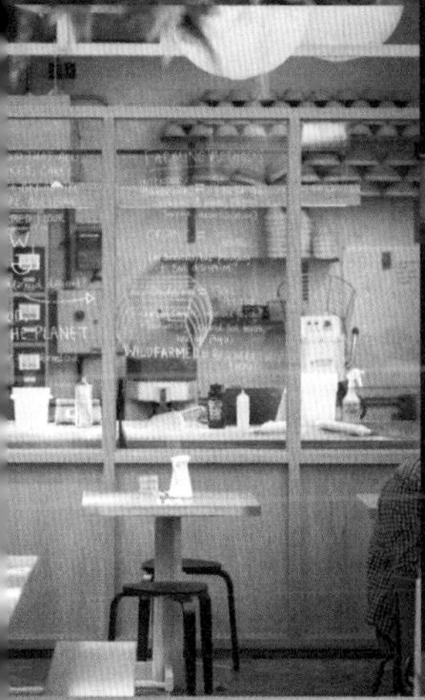
WILDFARMED

SORTING OFFICE

WILDFARMED
SOURDOUGH

LA MARZOCCO

BAKERY
COFFEE

Buttermilk Pancakes with Peanut Butter Custard and Miso Caramel

Preparation time: 20 minutes, plus 4 hours chilling | Cooking time: 40-50 minutes | Serves 4

Marmadukes' buttermilk pancakes have been a brunch staple since the opening of our flagship Norfolk Row café in August 2012. For this recipe, we've paired our thick, fluffy pancakes with one of our most popular French toast toppings from our third location and bakery, The Sorting Office.

For the crème diplomat

30g custard powder or cornflour

100g golden caster sugar

95g egg yolks & 400g whole milk

½ tsp vanilla paste

100g peanut butter

240ml double cream

For the miso caramel

170g butter

420g golden caster sugar

100ml water & 250g double cream

4 tbsp white miso

For the candied peanuts

100g peanuts

50g golden caster sugar & 10ml water

For the pancakes

300g plain flour & 3 tsp baking powder

½ tsp Maldon salt & 6 eggs

240ml buttermilk & 150ml cold water

To serve

2-4 bananas, sliced

For the crème diplomat

Start by making the crème patisserie base. In a large heatproof bowl, whisk the custard powder or cornflour with half of the sugar. Add the egg yolks and whisk until smooth. Heat the milk with the remaining sugar and vanilla until it starts to steam. Slowly pour the warmed milk onto the egg mixture while whisking until there is around a quarter of the milk left in the pan, then add the tempered egg mixture back to the pan and whisk to combine. Return the pan to a medium-low heat. Whisking constantly, heat until the mixture thickens to a smooth custard. Pass it through a fine sieve onto the peanut butter in a heatproof bowl. Leave for a moment to soften, then gently whisk together. Cover the surface of the custard with cling film to prevent a skin forming. Cool, then refrigerate for at least 4 hours. Whip the double cream until soft peaks form. Beat the chilled crème patisserie and then fold in the whipped cream.

For the miso caramel and candied peanuts

Heat the butter, sugar and water in a saucepan until honeycomb-coloured. Add the double cream and miso, then whisk until smooth. Toast the peanuts in the oven at 160°c fan for 10 minutes until lightly golden, then keep warm. Put the sugar into a non-stick saucepan and cover with the water, stirring to dissolve, then heat without stirring until it reaches a temperature of 118°c. Add the nuts and stir like crazy! The nuts will crystallise as they are agitated, but keep stirring and they will return to a golden caramel. Pour onto a parchment-lined baking tray and allow to set, then break up into clusters.

For the pancakes

Whisk the dry ingredients together in one bowl and the wet ingredients in another. Add together and whisk until smooth. Heat an oven to 120°c fan. Melt a little butter in a 6-inch round frying pan. Ladle a 1cm layer of pancake batter into the warm pan and cook until the edges of the pancake begin to set, before flipping to cook the other side. Tip the cooked pancake onto a parchment lined baking tray and place it in the oven to keep warm. Continue making pancakes with the remaining batter. To assemble, cut each pancake in half, and stack at angles on the serving plates. Add a heaped spoonful of peanut butter custard and drizzle generously with the warm miso caramel. Top with candied peanuts and fresh banana. Indulge!

MARMADUKES
x
WILDFARMED

This Girl Can

Based in Manchester's thriving Northern Quarter, Nibble is an independent café that's all about delicious and inclusive food with a generous helping of female empowerment.

Owner Lauren had always wanted a place of her own where she could bake and do things her way. She stumbled across the café at the right place and the wrong time but knew she had to make it work one way or another. Nibble was established in 2017 and has gone from strength to strength thanks to a team of five women, none of whom were trained chefs before working at the café, who all put a lot of love and determination into everything they do.

Nibble serves unpretentious brunch, lunch and cake with daily changing toasties such as the onion bhaji, curried cauliflower and mango chutney toastie which is one of Lauren's personal favourites. The brunch menu, updated seasonally with regular new specials, is extensive and includes things like the Ultimate Breakfast Bagel and Not Just Avocado on Toast. Everything is made in-house or sourced from local suppliers, including Grandad's Sausages, Kickback Coffee and bread from Barbakan Deli, all a short drive away from the café.

A huge part of Nibble's ethos is about offering options for everyone. They genuinely want a big group of people to come with all different dietary requirements, and for every single one of them to feel like they have the same great experience, with ample choice and great food that isn't missing anything. Catering for people with dietary requirements is never an afterthought at Nibble; there are always loads of vegan and gluten-free options for everyone to enjoy.

Located on Manchester's iconic Oldham Street, the café boasts an underground baking basement where the magic happens and an atmosphere that's super friendly, casual and female empowering. Lauren explains how important this is for Nibble, since she learnt on the job herself and trained up the women who work for her: "We couldn't do what we do if we didn't all pull our weight. We're a proper team and we all love each other."

The Covid-19 pandemic demanded yet more commitment and flexibility from the close-knit team, but they managed to keep Nibble going by pivoting the business online while the café had to close. Lauren is excited to grow that part of the business alongside serving breakfast and brunch in person; Nibble now offers UK delivery for their cakes, afternoon teas and loads more. They have even started a female empowerment merch line to help other women, and girls, believe that they can do absolutely anything.

YOU SURVIVED
THREE
ANYTHING!
GIRLS
FUCKING

nibble

always remember

Sweet Smoky Beans on Toast

Preparation time: 15 minutes | Cooking time: 1 hour | Serves 4+ (great for freezing)

I put these on the menu because my dad's a huge fan of proper beans on toast, slow cooked with proper ingredients and not full of preservatives and rubbish. They've been on the menu since day one, and you can serve them with anything!

For the beans

Light olive oil, for frying
1 medium white onion
3 sprigs of fresh thyme (or 1 tsp dried)
2 dried bay leaves
2 cloves of garlic
1 jar of roasted peppers
1 tin of whole plum tomatoes
1 vegetable stock pot
7g smoked paprika
30g dark brown sugar
1 tin of cannellini beans
1 tin of butter beans
1 tin of chickpeas (or beans/pulses of your choice)

To serve

2 avocados
1 lime & 1 red chilli
2 spring onions
Handful of fresh coriander
Bread of your choice
Butter or vegan spread

In a large pan, heat 1-2 tablespoons of olive oil on a medium heat (enough to coat the bottom of the pan). While this heats up, thinly slice the onion, then add it to the pan with the thyme and bay leaves. Season the onions with a little salt and sweat them off until soft.

Meanwhile, finely chop the garlic and thinly slice the roasted peppers. Once the onions are soft, add the garlic, peppers, tinned tomatoes, stock pot, paprika and sugar to the pan. Mix well and bring to a gentle simmer.

Cook the smoky tomato sauce for 20 minutes to intensify the flavours, then add salt and pepper to taste. Drain the beans and chickpeas, then stir them into the sauce. Bring the mixture back to a gentle simmer and cook for another 20 minutes on a low-medium heat, stirring occasionally to make sure nothing burns on the bottom of the pan. Season again to taste if needed.

While you're waiting for the beans, you can prep the toppings. Carefully slice the avocados in half around the stone and twist the halves until they separate. Remove the stone and slice the avocado horizontally within the skin. Slice vertically to create cubes, then scoop out into a bowl. Juice half the lime into the bowl, season with some salt and mix. Taste and add more lime juice if needed.

Thinly slice the chilli, spring onion and coriander, then combine in another bowl. When your beans are ready, toast your bread. There's no gluten in this recipe so it's great with gluten-free bread too. When the toast is done to your liking, butter it and then spoon your beans over the top. Add your avocado and then some of the spicy garnish. You can add other toppings too if you like; these beans go with everything! Try them with chorizo and goat's cheese, fried eggs and bacon, on the side of a fry up, with sausages and cheesy mash... the list is endless!

A Grand Day Out

Come for a candle-lit breakfast off the beaten track and stay for Oeuf's deliciously wholesome food amidst beautiful surroundings, just a stone's throw from the seafront in Hove.

When guests walk through the arched doorway into the grandeur of a Georgian townhouse, they know that an experience – not just breakfast or brunch – is on the menu. More than just a café, Oeuf is situated in the tranquil seaside resort of Hove, inside a beautiful old building that was lovingly renovated to bring founder Amber's longstanding vision to life. Soaring ceilings painted with celestial scenes, marble pillars and a gently crumbling interior needed plenty of TLC before the café could open in 2020. Despite the months of forced closures due to the pandemic that followed, Oeuf has already established itself as one of the city's favourite dining destinations.

For Amber and her team, your first meal of the day is the most important so it felt only right to turn that meal into an occasion, rather than something rushed or grabbed on the go. To that end, the café serves affordable yet hearty food with big flavours, drawing on the French-Moroccan influence that gave Oeuf its name. Many of the dishes lend themselves to sharing, adding to the relaxed atmosphere, and the signature Frumpets (French toast battered crumpets that can be sweet or savoury) have been a real hit with everyone since they were launched as a special, including some visitors who travelled from the US to try them!

From chicken and waffles to eggs Benedict, the menu is all about seasonal produce sourced with sustainability in mind. It's deliberately limited, ensuring that everything is made to the highest standards without waste, and kept fresh by head chef Kendal Cooper who has been instrumental in developing new dishes and bringing a wealth of experience to the kitchen.

With more than a decade of running restaurants behind her and a personal passion for breakfast and brunch, Amber knew she wanted to create somewhere that offered the excitement of something a little bit special, and her approach has proved very popular. She is now thinking about what they can give back having established themselves in the "hugely supportive" community, such as turning their used coffee grounds into compost for local gardens. However they move forward, Oeuf will continue building on its core ethos of making breakfast and brunch the focus of the day to be enjoyed in a beautiful setting by the sea.

Secret
Garden
Out Back

Oeuf.

Oeuf.

Oeuf and Surf

Preparation time: 10 minutes | Cooking time: 5 minutes | Serves 2-3

This dish was created due to us being close to the sea and using our local produce and suppliers. It was designed for a nice sunny summer's day, but we now add it to salads, baguettes and so many other dishes. It's such a tasty light dish that's full of flavour!

1 small red chilli, finely chopped

Small bunch of chives, finely chopped

2 spring onions, finely chopped

100g white crab meat, shelled

2 limes, zest of 1 and juice of both

Salt and pepper, to taste

20g white wine vinegar

4 eggs

2-3 slices of sourdough bread (or any of your preference)

20g butter, melted

Mix all the chopped ingredients with the crab meat, lime zest and juice, salt and pepper. Make sure you taste it and adjust the seasoning to your preference.

Put some water on to a rolling boil, and then add the white wine vinegar. Crack the eggs, one at a time, into the water and time for around 2½ to 3 minutes depending on the size of the egg and how you like them cooked. When they're done take them out and drain on a piece of kitchen roll.

To serve

Toast your sourdough bread and spoon on the crab mixture. Drizzle over the melted butter and place the poached eggs on top. Bon appetit!

Sandwiches and Socials

This neighbourhood café on Bishopthorpe Road in the centre of York focuses on excellent food prepared with top quality local produce and a friendly atmosphere designed to make people smile.

Steve and Julia opened The Pig & Pastry in June 2008, just as the financial crisis was deepening. Despite the difficult economic situation, the couple were settled in York with their kids and felt the time was right to embark on something together, as Julia had been a paediatric nurse and Steve a chef working for other people. The venture began as a delicatessen/café with an emphasis on baked goods, lending both the pig (for the deli) and the pastry (for the bakery) to its name. Today the café is a real community hub with a reputation for good food, freshly made with the best ingredients.

To this end, Steve and Julia buy as much as they can direct from the source. Meat is bought direct from a farm in Cold Kirby near Thirsk, and free-range milk in reusable glass bottles from the Dales. They also use Brunswick Organic Nursery for salad, fruit and veggies; local 'smokehouse guy' Justin Staal; Elliott's Eggs in the Yorkshire Wolds; Derwent Honey; and Short Stack Farm near Pocklington for grower Ben's amazing micro herbs and shoots. Haxby Bakehouse also makes the cut because although they make all their own bread otherwise, "nobody can beat Phil's sourdough."

With people from all walks of life – builders, artists, mums, students, pensioners, you name it – coming in for breakfast, brunch and lunch every day, The Pig & Pastry offers a daily changing specials board alongside the varied regular menu. This includes a proper fry up (very popular and available meaty or veggie) as well as breakfast sandwiches, eggs Benedict, and plenty of delicious things on toast. People can enjoy their food with a bit of company at sharing tables, which had to go during the pandemic but recently returned because Steve and Julia see "so many people out there whose only other human contact in the day is visiting a café or a shop. Let's make that visit a happy one."

The owners have had plenty of opportunity to open another branch during more than a decade of success with The Pig & Pastry but are very happy where they are, enjoying the creativity and connection with their community. As Steve puts it, "hats off to those that want to grow larger, but I remember a great line from Anthony Bourdain: too many cooks get delusions of grandeur, expanding their empire only to find their own personal Stalingrad waiting to greet them." No such delusions here, just good people and good food with a dash of good humour for every visitor.

Gluten Free
Blueberry &

Breakfast Burger

Preparation time: 20 minutes | Cooking time: 10 minutes | Serves 2

Everything you need between two bits of bread. It's messy, there's no easy way to eat it, and you'll need two hands and plenty of kitchen roll. P.S. There's no actual 'burger' because it's filled with all the best elements of a great brekkie.

For the relish

Olive oil

1 red onion, diced

1 white onion, diced

2 red chillies, finely sliced

2 cloves of garlic, finely sliced

1.25kg tomatoes, cut into eighths

300ml red wine vinegar

300g caster sugar

Salt and pepper

For the 'burgers'

2 heaped tsp smoky mayonnaise (see method)

½ avocado

2 bread rolls (ideally soft white baps)

4 rashers of dry cured back bacon

2 free-range eggs

2 slices of mature cheddar

2 tbsp homemade tomato relish

Handful of rocket salad (unless you have hands like shovels, then just make that half a handful)

First off, make the relish. Sweat the diced onions in a little olive oil until softened. Add the chilli, garlic and tomatoes, then allow to cook for 10-15 minutes. Stir in the vinegar and sugar, then simmer the relish for 30 minutes. Taste and season with salt and pepper as needed.

Strain the relish through a colander over a clean saucepan, keeping both the liquid and solids. Put the pan of liquid on a medium heat until reduced by half, then stir this back into the drained tomato mixture. Mix well and transfer to an airtight container. Keep chilled until needed.

Now make the smoky mayo by simply adding a little smoked paprika and ketchup to some mayonnaise. Prep the avocado by peeling off the skin and mashing the flesh with a fork, then add a little lemon juice and seasoning to taste.

Toast the bread rolls. We like to butter our buns, then sit them butter side down on a hot griddle or frying pan until golden. This gives you a nice crunch on the outside and a steamed pillowy soft texture on the inside.

Meanwhile, grill the bacon under a high heat until crispy and fry the eggs in a little oil, leaving the yolks nice and runny. Sit each cooked egg on top of 2 crispy bacon rashers, then cover with a slice of cheese and place the whole stack under the grill for about 30 seconds.

Now build the burgers. On the lids, a dollop of the smoky mayo and some rocket salad. On the bases, a spoonful of the mashed avo followed by a spoonful of your tomato relish, then the bacon-egg-cheese ensemble. Put the two halves together and enjoy!

Pudding Perfection

Driven by the desire to be their own bosses, Anthony and Emma have created a beautiful brunch experience in the heart of Nottingham. Whether it's a boozy brunch or afternoon tea, there's a tasty treat on the menu for everyone.

Having grown up in his parents' hotel, Anthony chose to pursue his dream of creating a cosy café experience, opting out of university to focus on his career. In support of her partner, Emma left her job as a teacher to dedicate herself to the success of The Pudding Pantry. Together, the pair have created one of the tastiest eateries in Nottingham. With three venues around the city, The Pudding Pantry is never too far away to satisfy any sweet cravings. Housed in an old pub, an old solicitor's office and a beautiful new build, each site boasts a relaxed, friendly atmosphere with The Pudding Pantry's signature turquoise interior so you can't miss it!

Since opening in 2014, the café has outgrown its namesake as a pudding shop and expanded to serve a wide variety of cakes and bakes. Incorporating influences from their travels around the world, Emma and Anthony have curated a bespoke menu that is constantly evolving. Seasonal changes make the best use of the freshest ingredients from their local market and special events like Mother's Day are catered to with beautiful brunches and homemade cakes.

Executive chef Luke keeps track of trends and successes, ensuring that tried-and-tested favourites are always available while other treats are rotated to provide a new experience on every visit. Being a small, independent business, the menu can easily be adapted to suit customer preferences, a feature which makes The Pudding Pantry a favourite for all.

Every dish is made from scratch and afternoon tea experiences are perfect for any special occasion. Going above and beyond for their local community, The Pudding Pantry also boasts a 'Pay It Forward' initiative, a charitable project aiming to make sure that no child goes hungry.

The team celebrated their 8th anniversary this year but they have no intention of stopping there. According to Anthony, the magic number of sites is five, a number that allows the pair control and brand recognition across every location without compromising on the passion behind the puddings. Hopefully, it won't be too long until we see another addition to The Pudding Pantry empire!

The PUDDING PANTRY
The PUDDING PANTRY

ice cream
vanilla
strawberries & cream
chocolate
salted caramel
mint choc chip
pistachio & almond
toffee & banana
snickers
cookies & cream

menu
LOADED cheesecake
→ salted caramel brownie
→ red velvet
→ Bakewell
COOKIE DOUGH
→ smores
→ cookies & cream
→ nutella
FLUFFERNUTTER

trillionaire

Mixed
BERRY

Pulled Hoisin Duck Pancakes

Preparation time: 15 minutes, plus marinating overnight | Cooking time: 3 hours | Serves 4

Created for Pancake Day by our executive chef Luke, this is a firm favourite amongst the team. Don't be put off by the long list of ingredients; this dish is absolutely worth the effort!

For the pulled duck

5g chopped garlic

3 star anise & 1 cinnamon stick

1 tbsp coriander seeds & ½ tbsp five spice

4 duck legs

300g goose fat or sunflower oil

For the hoisin sauce

12 tbsp soy sauce

6 tbsp smooth peanut butter

3 tbsp dark brown sugar

Tabasco sauce, to taste

1 large orange, juiced

For the pancakes

600g self-raising flour

2 tsp baking powder

50g caster sugar & 1 tsp salt

1 litre yoghurt & 6 eggs

100ml whole milk

To serve

4 fried eggs

Spring onions, thinly sliced

For the pulled duck

Mix the garlic, spices and 1 teaspoon each of salt and black pepper together in a bowl and rub over the duck legs. Cover and leave to marinate overnight. The next day, preheat the oven to 150°c. Pat the duck dry but don't remove the marinade. Place in a roasting tin and pour in the goose fat or oil until it just covers the duck legs. Place in the oven and cook for 2 hours 30 minutes.

In the meantime, make the hoisin sauce by blending all the ingredients together with half a teaspoon of black pepper. Once cooked, remove the duck from the pan and pull the meat off the bones. Mix the hoisin sauce into the pulled duck until fully coated.

For the pancakes

Mix the dry ingredients together, whisk the wet ingredients together, then combine the two to make a smooth batter. Heat a frying pan with a little oil or butter on a medium heat. Add a round dollop of the pancake mix – you should be able to get 3-4 of these in a pan – and wait until the batter starts to bubble on top. This should take a few minutes. Flip the pancakes over and cook for 3 more minutes on the other side. Transfer to a warm plate and repeat with the remaining batter.

To serve

Make a stack of 4 pancakes and place a big spoonful of the hoisin duck on top so that it falls down one side. Add a drizzle of hoisin sauce to the plate, then finish with a fried egg and sprinkle over some sliced spring onion.

A Foodie Family

Based in the charming historical city of Canterbury but just 20 minutes from the Kentish coastline, The Refectory Kitchen has a well-deserved reputation as one of the county's best breakfast spots.

Back in 2003, brothers Dan and Graham took on a sandwich shop in Canterbury. With parents who worked in the catering industry, they always aspired to do something more, which began with renovations to the beautiful 16th century building that housed their venture. Over time, original features were uncovered, and a large kitchen added, creating a space worthy of the restaurant that eventually became The Refectory Kitchen. Known for its fresh, homemade and locally sourced food across Kent, the all-day breakfast and brunch hotspot has also been featured in The New York Times, The Telegraph and 2020's Lonely Planet Guide!

The focus has been on breakfast and brunch since its transformation, as Dan and Graham enjoyed going out for the first meal of the day but wanted to bring the standard of food in line with any other daytime and evening establishment. They do this by offering a "clean menu" full of satisfying dishes that never rely on fried or tinned ingredients – one of their biggest sellers is the Grill Up – but instead feature things you wouldn't get at home or in a greasy spoon. From homemade baked beans, hash browns and jams to house-smoked bacon, salmon and mackerel, The Refectory Kitchen chefs go the extra mile to transform any humble breakfast into a real experience.

"We want people to have fun here," says Dan, "and that approach is reflected not only in our menu but in our quirky décor, right down to the artwork we choose to display and even the bespoke bar that a local architect designed for us." This individuality coupled with a real feeling of connection to their home city is the backbone of The Refectory Kitchen ethos. Whether it's sourcing sourdough from Docker, the bakery down the road, or welcoming returning customers who know the long-serving staff by name, the restaurant truly embodies the meaning of a family business.

Dan's partner Sophie joined them in 2020, bringing front of house management skills to the restaurant, and all three spend time on the floor to make sure they know the whole team and manage the business with as much passion as they started out with over a decade ago. They know they're getting something right when local Michelin-starred chefs line up to eat at The Refectory Kitchen! With a fantastic location just outside Canterbury's famous Westgate Towers – one of the country's largest surviving medieval gateways and a huge tourist attraction – breakfast or brunch at The Refectory Kitchen is not to be missed.

PEDS
MEOW
KATE
YUM
HAM
HERB
friends
EMILY

REFECTORY KITCHEN
EST 2012

The Refectory Rancher

Preparation time: 15 minutes | Cooking time: 15 minutes | Serves 4

While experimenting one Saturday morning before service, our team of chefs wanted to create something that included one ingredient each of them loved. Little did we know it would go on to become one of our bestselling and longest standing breakfast dishes!

600g sausage meat (we recommend using your favourite sausages with the skins removed)

2 avocados

1 lime

Salt and pepper

4 English muffins

8 large free-range eggs

8 large gem lettuce leaves

Fresh chives

For the hollandaise

2 egg yolks

7ml white wine vinegar

125g unsalted butter

1 tsp chipotle paste (or to taste if you prefer it a little spicier!)

Bring a pan of water containing a splash of white wine vinegar to a rolling boil. Meanwhile, shape your sausage patties into flat discs of about 75g each. In a bowl, smash the avocado with a squeeze of lime juice and season with salt and pepper to taste. Set this aside.

Lightly coat the bottom of a frying pan with oil and place over a medium-high heat. Once hot, add your sausage patties. These need to be cooked for 6 minutes on each side, until golden brown and cooked through.

While the patties are cooking, add the egg yolks and vinegar for the hollandaise to a large plastic measuring jug and blitz together on a medium-high speed with a stick blender.

Heat the butter in the microwave until it's melted and hot – you will know it's at the right temperature once it has split into the heavy fat at the bottom, and a clear liquid on top. You'll then need to blend the butter until it's combined again.

Using the stick blender on medium speed, slowly add the hot blended butter to the egg yolks and vinegar, blending until the ingredients are combined and you have a smooth and glossy consistency.

Add the chipotle paste to your hollandaise with the stick blender on a low speed and blitz until just combined (usually only around 5-10 seconds).

Slice the muffins in half and get them in the toaster. In the pan of boiling water, create a swirl using a large slotted spoon and then gently crack the eggs in one by one, keeping the water swirling as best you can, and poach for 3 minutes.

To serve

Place a lettuce leaf on each half of the toasted muffin, followed by your hot sausage patty.

Add a dessert spoon of the smashed avocado. Create a little well in the avocado and place a poached egg on top. You can then add a generous helping of the chipotle hollandaise sauce on top, and garnish with freshly chopped chives.

Rise & Shine

Putting all day brunching back on the menu, Rise has been so well received in Preston that a second branch has opened in York.

When Leigh and Jack worked together in bars and restaurants, they sought an all-day brunch in a vibrant venue with attentive service. They found that most places stopped serving the best meal of the day too early, in contrast to many countries around the world they had travelled to. The co- workers turned co-founders wanted to create somewhere that served brunch all day, in aesthetically pleasing venues, so in October 2019 they opened Rise in Preston!

They chose Preston as it was between their hometowns and had a gap in the market for what they were offering, which proved to be a great location and quickly became popular. Despite having to close just months later in March 2020 because of the Covid-19 pandemic, Leigh and Jack were undaunted and created a takeaway offering. Also, during this time they focused on social media marketing, which has resulted in thousands of Instagram followers.

"What sets us apart is that we aim to smash all three bases: awesome service, great food and reasonable prices," explains Leigh. "We do a lot of training with our staff and have great retention as they love working here, including the chefs who get lots of creative licence which attracts some fantastic talent." Having worked in the restaurant industry for years, both business partners have insider knowledge when it comes to suppliers too, so they avoid the middleman when sourcing the freshest local produce.

Leigh's close friend and head chef Connor is responsible for turning these ingredients into delicious dishes; he designs the menu with input from the rest of the team, including weekly specials for each location and new additions every few months. Staples like the breakfast rolls and All Rise stick around though, and there are always alternatives available for those with allergies such as gluten-free sourdough.

Rise Preston is housed in a Grade II listed Arcade and the newer addition on Fossgate in York is a stone's throw from the famous Shambles shopping street. It's not just the food that makes Rise something special. Sustainability is just as important as the detail in every aesthetic, with bamboo straws in their cold drinks which are a massive hit with the regulars, and the menus are printed on recycled coffee cups. The freshly made food, coffee and smoothies are guaranteed to bring you a bit of sunshine at any time of day.

Top right photo: Rachel Ovenden

Wild Mushrooms with Ricotta and Butternut Ketchup

Preparation time: 10 minutes | Cooking time: 5 minutes | Serves 2

We run weekend specials throughout the year and our most popular then make it onto our menu when we make seasonal changes. This dish was a popular special and just had to come on our menu due to people power!

For the butternut ketchup

½ butternut squash
1 small onion
1 clove of garlic
1 fresh chilli
20g brown sugar
20ml white wine vinegar
1 sprig of tarragon

For the ricotta

125g ricotta
½ unwaxed lemon
Pinch of chopped chives

To serve

2 tbsp olive oil
250g wild mushrooms, chopped
Butter
1 clove of garlic, minced
Pinch of tarragon
2 handfuls of kale
2 slices of thick cut sourdough
Fresh coriander

For the butternut ketchup

Peel and dice the butternut squash into 1cm cubes, place in an ovenproof tray lined with tin foil and roast in the oven at 170°c for around 20 minutes until the butternut has softened.
Finely chop the onion, garlic and chilli and then sweat them for 5 minutes in a frying pan. Add the cooked butternut, brown sugar, white wine vinegar and tarragon. Bring to the boil and reduce by half. Finally, blitz until smooth to make a ketchup.

For the ricotta

Mix the ricotta with the zest and juice of the lemon half, a large pinch of chives, and salt and pepper to taste.

To serve

Preheat a frying pan on a medium-high heat, add the olive oil and fry the mushrooms until fully cooked through. Add a small knob of butter with the garlic and tarragon. Season with salt and pepper. Toss the kale in some oil and heat in a pan or in the oven for a few minutes until crispy. Toast the sourdough lightly on each side.
Swirl the butternut ketchup on a plate as a bed for your toast, add a couple of tablespoons of the ricotta mix and spoon the wild mushrooms on top. Add some extra butternut ketchup (use a squeezy bottle if you have one) and place the crispy kale on top, and then garnish with some extra lemon zest and fresh coriander to finish. Bon appétit!
Chef's Tip: add a poached egg or two for those who like a runny yolk!

rise.

Stirring Things Up

Whether you have a hankering for a bacon butty or a longing for something sweet, Stir has tasty treats to satisfy the whole family.

Since opening its doors in 2015, Stir has grown into an end-to-end café that continues to impress. The concept was the brainchild of Judith Harrison, an entrepreneur who was determined to create a cosy place in the community where locals and visitors alike could relax with a cup of coffee.

Beginning from just a name in a young mum's mind, Stir has become a recognisable brand in Cambridge which delivers the highest quality food and award-winning bread recipes. The venture has since expanded to include a further site, a food van and a bakery which serves each venue as well as selling fresh loaves directly to the public. With such a variety of venues, each space has its own vibe and appeal, ranging from industrial chic adorned with art from local creatives to a quirky van in the middle of a historic urban oasis.

With no prior experience running an eatery, Judith's success comes from her drive to learn and grow alongside her amazing team at each venue. One of the team's most notable successes to date is head baker Veronika being awarded Britain's Best Gluten-Free Loaf 2022 by the British Baking Awards for her yummy smoked beetroot and chilli jam loaf.

By baking all of their own bread in their own bakery, Stir can cater to everyone and the menu is regularly changed to make the best use of seasonal ingredients. With tried and tested favourites available all year round alongside a rotating menu of fresh ingredients and ideas, there's always something delicious on offer at Stir.

Customers can recreate their favourites at home with the coffee beans, spreads and gift boxes available or give back to the community by donating loaves to the local foodbank. If you're after something sweet, you can stock up on their tasty treats like millionaire's shortbread or vegan flapjacks. If you're looking for something convenient and delicious, Stir also offer bread subscriptions that are delivered right to your door! Whether it's a Sunday stroll and a bacon roll or big brunch and a cocktail, Stir has a little something for everyone.

ST/R
LOCAL·SOCIAL·CB4

ST/R
ST/R
ST/R
This cup is fully recyclable

Berry Bostock

Preparation time: 20 minutes (unless you're making your own bread!) | Cooking time: 20 minutes | Serves 4

Traditionally made as a way to use up stale brioche bread, the beautiful Bostock is a cross between French toast and an almond croissant. Our bakers make the brioche loaves fresh but if you haven't time to do this, you can use shop-bought brioche or even a good quality thickly sliced white bread.

For the syrup

1 large orange

70g caster sugar

1 tbsp water

For the frangipane

125g unsalted butter, at room temp

160g caster sugar

2 medium eggs

200g ground almonds

1 tsp each almond & vanilla essence

For the compote

100g sugar

100g each blueberries & raspberries

1 tbsp water

To assemble

4 large slices of brioche

100g flaked almonds

Icing sugar, to serve

1 large dollop of quality Greek yoghurt

1 handful of blueberries and raspberries

1 sprig of mint, for garnish

Preheat the oven to 180°c (160°c fan) and line your baking tray with baking parchment.

For the syrup
To make the syrup, juice the orange and put in a small saucepan with the sugar and water. Pare strips of zest from the orange peel and add to the saucepan, bringing it to the boil. Let it simmer for a bit and, when the syrup is a good consistency, set it aside to cool.

For the frangipane
Beat the butter and sugar together, and then stir in the remaining ingredients. Beat for another minute or so until the mixture is well combined. Set aside.

For the compote
In another saucepan, combine the sugar, berries and water. Bring to the boil and simmer until the mixture has thickened.

To assemble
Assemble the Bostock by laying out the thick slices of brioche on the baking parchment and brushing each slice evenly with the orange syrup. Continue to do this until the syrup is used up. Spoon the compote on to each slice, spreading to the very edge of the bread and then spread the frangipane on top. Again, spread it right to the edge of the bread. Sprinkle the almonds on top of each slice.
Place the tray in the oven and bake for around 20 minutes, or until the frangipane is a golden brown colour. Let the slices cool slightly for 5 minutes or so and dust each slice with the icing sugar.
Serve each on a separate plate with a dollop of Greek yoghurt, berries on the side and a sprig of mint on top for garnish.

Beach Bum Brunches

Set yourself up for a glorious day on the golden sands of Gwithian with a hearty breakfast and Cornish coffee from this beautiful beachfront café.

Having previously owned a successful hotel and restaurant, opening Sunset Surf was the natural next step for Annabelle and Graham. After running their business for twelve years, the café was a way to step back and embrace the laid-back Cornish lifestyle while still curating a beautiful eating experience. Swapping late nights behind the bar for bright mornings and breakfasts, the team at Sunset Surf serve up a tasty start to every day.

Set on the most beautiful stretch of Cornish coastline, Sunset Surf boasts some of the most amazing panoramas to enjoy over a hot coffee. From the terrace, you can fully appreciate the views over the sandy dunes and clear expanse of ocean below, the gentle rush of waves a permanent soundtrack to this beachfront café, bar and surf hire.

With complete focus on family and community, this café showcases some of the best local produce on offer, using fresh meat from Harvey Brothers Butchers and eggs from up the road at Cornhill Farm. The pair pride themselves on their community spirit, focusing on the importance of looking after their staff, customers and other local business owners. With patrons who return year upon year like long-lost friends, the team's friendly spirit is evident through their impeccable service.

When asked if there were any favourites on the menu, Annabelle explained that everything on the menu is fantastic and wouldn't be there otherwise! With something for the surfers, the kids and the picky eaters, there is a tasty treat available for everyone. On warm days, you can wash it down with a homemade milkshake or smoothie, all made using a plethora of Cornish produce. While the main menu stays the same, the devil is in the details. Chefs Ash and Liam curate the menu around seasonal availability and their passion for food is evident in every dish. With gluten-free and veggie options available, Sunset Surf can cater to all.

After breakfast, sign yourself up for surf lessons or enjoy some Cornish ice cream on the beach. Head over to their website to access the Surfline webcam and check the waves while you eat! For those even more eager to fully embrace the relaxed atmosphere of the coastline, Sunset Surf also features a beautifully furbished 1-bed flat which is nestled just five minutes from the beach. With everything available to take away, why not enjoy your breakfast on the golden dunes this summer?

TRX 424D
MCY 42E

SUNSET SURF

CAFE

SURF
CLUB

Surfers Special Breakfast

Preparation time: 10 minutes | Cooking time: 20 minutes (less if you come into the café and order it!) | Serves 2

When you have just come in from an early morning surf and need refueling, this dish will do the trick. We recommend Harvey Brothers Butchers for all the meat but feel free to use your local butchers! This dish showcases hog's pudding - a very traditional West Country sausage which is spicier than a white sausage.

2 sausages
2 vine tomatoes
2 Portobello mushrooms
Butter
Salt and pepper
2 thick slices of hog's pudding
2 thick slices of black pudding
4 rashers of bacon (of your choice)
2 free-range eggs
1 tin of Heinz beans

Turn the oven on to a medium heat in preparation to cook your sausages. Pop them on a baking tray with a drizzle of oil and cook for 10 minutes.

Next, halve your tomatoes and add them into the oven with the sausages.

Remove the stalks from the mushrooms and gently fry the heads in a frying pan with butter. Season with salt and pepper to taste.

Lastly, add the slices of hog's pudding and black pudding to the baking tray. Once the sausages and puddings have browned, lower the oven temperature and leave the ingredients to rest.

To prepare the bacon, warm a pan over a medium heat and cook the rashers until they are sizzling.

Gently lower the heat and crack in the eggs, adding a small knob of butter if necessary. Lightly baste the eggs to cook the tops.

When the meat and eggs are nearly cooked, heat up your baked beans in a separate pan. Serve everything on a warm platter with toast and butter.

Kiwi Cuisine

Inspired by the great café scene in New Zealand, business partners Natalie and Jon decided to bring back some Kiwi cuisine to British soil.

Housed in a white-washed 19th century former silversmiths in the heart of Sheffield's Cultural Industries Quarter, Tamper Sellers Wheel began welcoming the people of Sheffield through their doors in 2011. Inside, the café boasts a simplistic décor, with old school chairs and work bench tables giving the place a nice rustic vibe that's complemented by the exposed red bricks and original vaulted ceilings. Paying homage to the business' motherland, a large mural of New Zealand's flora and fauna also occupies one of the café's walls, emphasising the Kiwi influences behind the business. In the bustling but friendly atmosphere, customers can sample some tasty classics from the land down under including Tamper's salt beef Benedict and the roasted squash and corn fritters, while mince 'n' toast is always a best seller too.

For those that enjoy a little boost to their day, the café has cakes and pastries freshly baked on the daily, and a house espresso blend from their very own tailored recipe. Customers can also hire out the venue, for evenings, parties, wedding receptions and corporate events. To top it off, they regularly host chef's nights, a popular occasion where the head chef designs a one-off seasonal menu for an interesting and different dining experience.

As well as seasonal menu changes, the chef often finds new and interesting ways to keep customers coming back for more, like taking inspiration from Australasian cafés and restaurants. With a great team of staff behind them, each and every one of them making themselves invaluable to the business, it's easy to see why Tamper pride themselves on a trifecta of great service, food, and coffee. They also value their relationships with the very best local suppliers who themselves champion quality, provenance, and seasonality. All their food is sourced and prepared fresh to provide you with the boldest and cleanest flavours.

At Tamper, they believe word of mouth is more powerful than any accolade. Even with a few awards under their belt, and an honourable mention in the national publication of the Sunday Telegraph, they like to attribute a lot of their success to the community and the many people behind the business that keep it thriving. As they say in New Zealand, kia ora – welcome!

NEW ZEALAND
EST. 2011
TAMPER

Tamper's Turkish Eggs

Preparation time: 40 minutes, plus overnight straining | Cooking time: 10-15 minutes | Serves 4

Roasted vegetables are a great addition to this indulgent brunch – we like Cajun-spiced butternut squash – and a few sliced chillies go really well for those who like a little extra heat.

For the strained yoghurt

500g natural yoghurt

2 cloves of garlic, finely chopped (or ½ tsp garlic purée)

½ tsp salt

For the dukkha

50g hazelnuts

1 tbsp cumin seeds

1 tbsp coriander seeds

1 tbsp sesame seeds

1 tbsp nigella seeds

½ tbsp fennel seeds

1 tsp ground turmeric

Pinch of salt and pepper

To serve

50ml white wine vinegar

8 eggs

1 bag of spinach, washed

1 medium leek, sliced

100g butter, plus extra for frying

Sliced focaccia or sourdough, toasted

Prepare the strained yoghurt and dukkha the night before. Mix the natural yoghurt, chopped garlic or purée and salt together. Put a colander inside a bowl, then line it with a 30 by 30cm muslin cloth or cheesecloth. Place the yoghurt in the cloth, cover with cling film and then let it sit for 12-16 hours overnight.

Preheat the oven to 180°c. Place all the dukkha ingredients on a baking tray and mix. Put the tray in the oven for 10-12 minutes, stirring halfway through. Take the tray out of the oven and leave to cool. Once cooled, place the mix in a food processor and blitz. Alternatively, you could use a pestle and mortar to grind them.

When you're ready to make the dish, scoop the strained yoghurt out of the muslin cloth into a container and set aside in the fridge.

To serve

Place a large saucepan of water on to boil and add the white wine vinegar. When the water has come to a rolling boil, turn it down to a simmer. With a slotted spoon give the water a stir to make a swirling current. Crack the eggs into the water and poach for 2-2½ minutes each. To get the best results, only have 4 eggs (maximum) in the saucepan at once. When cooked, but still soft, get them out and drain on a bit of cloth.

You can prepare your greens at the same time as your eggs. Place a frying pan over a high heat, adding a knob of butter when hot enough. Add a splash of olive oil with the spinach and leeks, seasoning accordingly, and allow the greens to wilt down.

When the eggs and greens are ready, put a dollop of yoghurt in each bowl and spread around the inside with a tablespoon. Place the greens into the middle of the bowl with 2 poached eggs on top. Put the 100g of butter into the frying pan that had the greens in with1 tablespoon of dukkha spice and let it melt down and foam. Spoon the dukkha butter over the eggs. Repeat this process for each dish and then serve them with the toasted focaccia or sourdough. Tuck in!

Hospitality with Personality

Marc Smith remembers a time when Stockton Heath only had one, maybe two restaurants. Almost 40 years later, the area is now known as Warrington's mecca for hospitality, a place bustling with activity. At the heart of it all, you'll find Terrace Bistro.

Having worked in hotels for most of his life, Marc is no novice when it comes to service. One of his first jobs was in a terrace restaurant in Daresbury, where the fine dining scene blew him away – his young mind was in awe of all this fancy food and the possibilities it presented. When it came to opening his own place, he wanted something a bit more relaxed so, in 2019, he opened Terrace Bistro. Inside, customers are met with an interior made up of bar tops, blue tones and coppers, all accompanied by a warm atmosphere to help make customers feel right at home.

The aim was to create a space with a vibrant, fun and welcoming environment: somewhere you could go to feel like you were being greeted by friends. The result has been just that. Marc can often be found front of house, spending most of his time chatting with customers. Phil Daley, head chef and director, will also happily come out from the kitchen and speak to customers about their food. Everyone goes out of their way to make it as enjoyable and memorable an experience as they can. This includes changing components of the dishes to suit the customers' dietary needs, or even just their preferences; if you can't decide between two of the eggs Benedict dishes then Phil will simply split it – one half Rueben and the other half Royale, for example.

Terrace's eggs are definitely a winner, with their Rueben's Egg Benedict (recipe included in this chapter!) being the absolute favourite amongst customers. The Corned Beef Eggs Benedict goes down a storm too. To keep things fresh, the menu changes every two months and is always dependent on the best ingredients available at the time. Most of Terrace's produce is sourced locally, with some of their ingredients even being made in house, like their hash browns, black pudding, and bread. The entire contents of their cheeseboards are sourced within a 50-mile radius of their front doorstep, the herbs and vegetables from Growing Field 28 in Daresbury, meat from the butchers only seven doors down – A. Ward & Son, and the fish from Warrington Market.

At Terrace, they believe the key to success is to keep customers at the forefront of everything. A sweet and simple ethos – one that's obviously working. As Marc says, "it isn't rocket science; it's what hospitality should look like – proper hospitality." Go and experience some for yourself!

TERRACE
BISTRO
49

Rueben's Eggs Benedict

Preparation time: 10 minutes | Cooking time: 20-25 minutes | Serves 4

New and improved, this is just one of Terrace's takes on the classic eggs Benedict and is a definite favourite among customers. Now you can try it at home!

250g butter
4 egg yolks
5ml white wine vinegar, plus extra for poaching
Lemon juice
2 gherkins, chopped
2 plum tomatoes, chopped
10ml tomato sauce
8 eggs, fridge cold
4 slices of rye bread
1 jar of sauerkraut
1 packet of sliced pastrami

Over a low heat, melt the butter in a saucepan, skimming any white solids from the surface. Keep the butter warm. In a different saucepan, put some water on to a gentle simmer. Add the egg yolks and white wine vinegar to a metal bowl and place on the saucepan, over the simmering water. Whisk the mixture until pale and thick. Remove the bowl from the heat and slowly add the melted butter until fully incorporated, then add a squeeze of lemon juice and salt to taste (if it gets too thick, add a splash of water). Finally, add the gherkins, chopped tomatoes and tomato sauce. Keep the hollandaise sauce warm while you prepare the rest of the dish.

For the poached eggs, bring a pan of water to the boil and add a good splash of the white wine vinegar. One at a time, crack your fridge-cold eggs into the boiling water and poach over a low heat for 3 minutes. Don't put more than 3 or 4 eggs in at once, depending on the size of your saucepan, so as not to overcrowd the water. When the eggs are done, drain and put them on a paper towel to dry.

To assemble

Toast the rye bread slices and add 5g of sauerkraut and 15g of the pastrami onto each slice. Place two eggs on each and add the thousand island hollandaise sauce over the top. To finish, garnish to your liking (we use delicious pea shoots) and enjoy a taste sensation to set you up for the day!

Pancakes & Poetry

Pioneering pancakes in the heart of London, Where The Pancakes Are serves up the very best stacks with an innovative approach to flavour and something for the whole family to enjoy.

For Where The Pancakes Are founder Patricia Trijbits, it all started on a cold, rainy day with a visit to a pancake place in London, her adopted home after the Netherlands, France and the US. With two toddlers in tow, she struggled to find somewhere the whole family would enjoy and realised what the city was missing... great pancakes! As her children grew up, Patricia decided to make her business idea a reality and opened the first branch near Borough Market at the end of 2016, followed by Charlotte Street in 2021 and Battersea Power Station hot on its heels in 2022.

Knowing that many diners, like herself, find comfort in the familiarity of their favourite haunts, Patricia and her expert team have replicated the award-winning menu in each location. Every pancake they serve is created with either the fermented buttermilk or vegan and gluten-free batter, both prepared from scratch without a blender in sight, something that Patricia takes great pride in. Using a wide range of beautiful ingredients to reflect a broad customer base, Where The Pancakes Are has been on Conde Nast's list of Top Ten Brunch Places in London since 2018 and also topped the list of family-friendly London eateries in 2022.

There are seasonal updates to the menu throughout the year: spring/summer sees Australian sweetcorn fritters topped with avocado replacing the autumn/winter staple of Welsh rarebit, made with locally brewed ale, for example. The biggest hit is always The American though: buttermilk pancakes with pure Québécois maple syrup and smoked streaky bacon from a butcher in North Yorkshire who delivers to them twice a week for the freshest produce. With such attention to quality, it's no wonder that more than two thirds of Patricia's customers become regulars. As her mother would say, the proof is in the pudding!

Inspired by Patricia's love of literature (the business name itself is a nod to famous children's book Where The Wild Things Are) these foodie destinations are planning to host a quarterly event called Pancakes & Page Turners, where book discussions are led by a guest speaker. Where The Pancakes Are also launched an online shop during the first nationwide lockdown, which features gift boxes containing speciality pancake mixes, signature ingredients and poetry books. This has gone from strength to strength since Patricia and her daughter delivered the first orders all over the country themselves, and the plan is to continue expanding their unique offering with more locations, not just across London but throughout the UK.

WHERE THE PANCAKES ARE

WHERE THE PANCAKES ARE
FLAT IRON SQUARE

Savoury
WHERE THE PANCAKES ARE

WHERE THE PANCAKES ARE
London's fave app
for groceries on tap
Welcome

Asparagus and Goat's Cheese Dutch Baby

Preparation time: 10 minutes | Cooking time: 20 minutes | Serves 2

Dutch Babies are an American reinvention of a northern German (Deutsch) pancake tradition, where the pancake batter is poured into an ovenproof cast iron pan and oven baked. Deutsch became Dutch and the rest is history!

5 eggs
292ml milk
208g plain flour
5g sugar
2g salt
20g butter
6 stems of poached asparagus, cut into 2-3cm pieces
200g Montgomery cheese, cubed
100g goat's cheese, roughly chopped
4 sprigs of thyme
2 sprigs of rosemary

For the side salad

Handful of rocket
Handful of shaved fennel
Balsamic dressing

Preheat the oven to 220°c and heat up two 8 inch round skillet pans. Whisk the eggs and milk together. In a separate bowl, combine the flour, sugar and salt.

Pour the dry mix into the wet mix and whizz with a hand blender until there are no lumps left.

Once the skillet is hot, add half the butter to each pan and swirl until it stops sizzling. Quickly add half the batter (approx. 200g) and half the asparagus to each pan. Place the pans into the oven.

After 10 minutes, the batter will have started to rise and crisp up. Remove the pans from the oven and scatter half of the cheese and herbs (sticking straight up) in the middle of each Dutch baby.

Cook for 15 more minutes and then serve piping hot with a simple side salad. We suggest rocket, shaved fennel and balsamic dressing.

Tuck in and enjoy!

T DEO

H ICR

E RTY

5TARA
139-141 Duke Street
Sheffield
S2 5QL
07440 620792
5tarasheffield139@gmail.com
www.5tara.co.uk
@5tara_sheffield
Cultural and traditionally authentic Punjabi cuisine, served with love and respect!

AESTHETE COFFEE + KITCHEN
348-352 South Road
Walkley
Sheffield
S6 3TE

52a Sandygate Road
Crosspool
Sheffield
S10 5RY
0114 232 2000
www.aesthetesheffield.com
@aesthete_sheffield
Independent mother and daughter establishment, serving delicious home cooked food using fresh ingredients, covering breakfast and lunch every day of the week.

THE BUS CAFÉ
The Sun Deck
Royal Crescent Promenade
Margate
Kent
CT9 5AJ
hello@thebuscafe.co.uk
www.thebuscafe.co.uk
@thebuscafe
Independent award-winning breakfast café based in a vintage double decker bus on Margate seafront.

CAFÉ MANGO'S
Kings Wharf
The Quay
Exeter
EX2 4AN
@mangosexeter
Small, unique café situated in the heart of Exeter's historic Quayside. Open 7 days a week from 9am, we offer up hearty brunches, healthy lunches and evening nibbles and cocktails.

THE CANTEEN
Broad Street
Old Portsmouth
PO1 2FS
023 9235 1935
info@thecanteen.co.uk
www.thecanteen.co.uk
@canteenhotwalls
Family-run waterfront eatery in beautifully restored historic barracks, with an outside deck overlooking The Solent. We serve all day brunch, lunch and an abundance of baked goods. Open 7 days a week, 8am - 4pm, with an Ice Cream Hut in the summer months.

CARAMELLO
762 Wilmslow Road
Didsbury
Manchester
M20 6UB
0161 823 7242
hello@caramelloofdidsbury.com
www.caramellodidsbury.co.uk
@caramellodidsbury
Artisan café serving all-day homemade breakfast, brunch, patisseries, Italian gelato, pancakes, waffles and coffee. We use the finest locally sourced fresh produce, with everything on the menu made fresh in-house.

CLOCKWORKS
11 Wolstenholme Square
Ropewalks
Liverpool
L1 4JJ
0151 7070 210
info@clockworksliverpool.net
www.clockworksliverpool.net
@clockworksliverpool
We offer breakfast, lunch and dinner, specialising in twisted British classics. We stick to what we do well: classic food and cocktails. Our food is often a little indulgent, but always comforting, tasty and entirely traceable. The way food should be. Independently owned and dedicated in supplying great food and drink to kickstart the Wolstenholme rejuvenation.

THE CRAFTY EGG
113 Stokes Croft
Bristol
BS1 3RW
thecraftyegg@gmail.com
@thecraftyegg
Independent coffee mongers serving up interesting recipes and delicious coffee for brunch lovers in a casual plant-lush setting.

CRWST
Priory Street
Cardigan
Ceredigion
SA43 1BU
www.crwst.cymru
@crwst.cymru
Brunch café located in the heart of Aberteifi (Cardigan) passionate about all things food, coffee and service. We take pride in making everything from scratch, from sourdough loaves and crispy hash browns to fluffy pancakes and caramel sauce!

CUP TEA SALON

9 Little Belmont Street
Aberdeen
AB10 1JG
www.cupteasalon.com

Cute, bustling, city centre tea salon with plentiful brunch options and delicious afternoon tea. Outdoor seating too. Open 7 days a week. Come and see us!

DUSTY'S KITCHEN

07984030240
info@jakemorley.co.uk
www.dustyskitchen.co.uk
@dustys2020

Our mission is to provide a little haven of tranquillity in a hectic world. We like to keep things simple: great coffee, good food, good vibes.

EAT ME CAFÉ

Stephen Joseph Theatre
Westborough
Scarborough
YO11 1JW
www.eatmecafe.com
@eatmecafe

Multi-award-winning café serving an eclectic mix of British and Asian food with a hint of so much more, situated within Scarborough's renowned theatre in-the-round.

EZRA & GIL

20 Hilton Street
Manchester
M1 1FR
hello@ezraandgil.co.uk
www.ezraandgil.com
@ezraandgil

Good food, good coffee, good people.

FITZBILLIES

51-52 Trumpington Street
Cambridge
CB2 1RG

36 Bridge Street
Cambridge
CB2 1UW
www.fitzbillies.com
@fitzbillies

Fitzbillies has been famous for its ultra-sticky Chelsea buns since 1920. The original, 100-year-old cake shop continues to operate behind its beautiful Art Nouveau facade on Trumpington Street, selling an amazing array of cakes to eat in or takeaway. The large café/restaurant, behind the cake shop, serves breakfast, lunch, brunch, coffee, traditional English afternoon tea, cakes and of course the famous buns, seven days a week. A trip to Cambridge isn't complete without a visit.

THE GOOD EGG

93 Church Street
Stoke Newington
N16 0AS
020 7682 2120

Kingly Court
Kingly Street
Soho
W1B 5PW
020 3911 2000
soho@thegoodegg.co / stokey@thegoodegg.co
www.thegoodegg.co
@thegoodegg_

Independent all-day restaurants serving up dishes inspired by the flavours of the Middle East, with nods to the cuisine of Tel Aviv's street food stalls, the fare sold in classic Jewish delis, grand old cafés, appetizing stores and the bagel bakeries of New York and Montreal.

THE GREEN ROCKET

1 Pierrepont Street
Bath
BA1 1LB
www.thegreenrocket.co.uk
@greenrocketcafe

Proudly independent and multi-award-winning café and restaurant in the centre of Bath. We provide tasty, fresh, vibrant, plant-based food and great coffee in an informal setting.

THE GRIND CAFÉ

3 Green Lane
Sheffield
S3 8SJ
01142723929
hello@grindcafe.co.uk
@thegrindcafesheffield

Expertly brewed coffee, carefully crafted cocktails, tasty treats baked on-site daily, and a delicious menu bursting with flavour.

HANKY PANKY

20 Commonhall Street
Chester
CH1 2BJ
01244 319225
hppancakes@live.com
www.hankypankypancakes.com
@hppancakes

HPHQ, in the heart of Chester, brings you a festival of flavour: delicious breakfasts, brunches, lunches and a dollop of fun any time of day!

HARTLEY FARM SHOP & KITCHEN

Winsley
Bradford on Avon
BA15 2JB
www.hartley-farm.co.uk
@hartleyfarm

Fifth generation family farm sourcing directly from local farmers, growers and makers to provide our customers with great quality, local and seasonal food and drink. We support a food system that values the quality of produce, the effort and care of the maker and the positive impacts on our community and environment.

HONEY + HARVEY

Riduna Park
Melton
Woodbridge
Suffolk
IP12 1QT

56 Thoroughfare
Woodbridge
Suffolk
IP12 1AL

5 Princes Street
Ipswich
Suffolk
IP1 1PH
@honeyandharvey

Small group of cafés/restaurants based in Suffolk, offering delicious breakfast, brunch and lunch. We use as many local ingredients as possible and roast our coffee in-house from our roastery based in Winchester.

LA HOGUE FARM SHOP & CAFÉ

Chippenham
Ely
CB7 5PZ
www.lahogue.co.uk
@lahoguefarm

Farm shop with onsite butchery and large café serving delicious home-cooked breakfasts, light lunches and amazing homemade cakes and desserts.

LYKKE

11 New Era Square
Sheffield
S2 4RB
0114 312 3710
info@wearelykke.com
www.wearelykke.com
@lykkesheffield

A new concept venue that opened in August 2021, proudly situated in New Era Square. Serving a delicious variety of coffees and cocktails, with brunch and pizza.

MARMADUKES

The Sorting Office
846 Ecclesall Road
S11 8TP

22 Norfolk Row
Sheffield
S1 2PA

42 Cambridge Street
Sheffield
S1 4HP
hello@marmadukes.co
www.marmadukes.co
@marmadukescafe

Our mission is to create a better all-day brunch experience, built around design-led spaces, best-in-class produce (particularly our speciality coffee and our own handmade bread, pastries and cakes), passionate, knowledgeable staff and a sustainable approach that empowers people and helps the planet.

NIBBLE

36 Oldham Street
Manchester
M1 1JN
0161 923 4845
cafe@nibblenq.com
www.nibblenq.com
@nibble_nq

We are a female-run independent café, small in size but big in personality. We are also an online shop with UK delivery of all our handmade cakes and 'girls can' merch line to help empower other women.

OEUF CAFÉ

8 Third Avenue
Hove
BN3 2PX
www.oeuf.cafe
@oeuf.cafe

Come for a candle-lit breakfast off the beaten track. Locally sourced food and drink amongst a setting of grandeur.

THE PIG & PASTRY

35 Bishopthorpe Road
York
YO23 1NA
01904 675133
thepigandpastryuk@gmail.com
www.thepigandpastry.com
@thepigandpastry_2.0

Neighbourhood café since 2008. We serve breakfast, brunch, lunch, sandwiches, salads, daily changing specials, home baking, relationship advice, TripAdvisor bribes and more…

THE PUDDING PANTRY

27/29 Trinity Square
Nottingham
NG1 4AF

579 Mansfield Road
Sherwood
NG5 2JN

83 High Road
Beeston
NG9 2LE
0115 960 4888 ext. 1
info@thepuddingpantry.co.uk
www.the puddingpantry.co.uk

We are a small, passionate team who pride ourselves on providing you with delicious, homemade food and friendly, personal service.

THE REFECTORY KITCHEN

16 St Dunstans Street
Canterbury
Kent
CT2 8AF
01227 638766
info@refetorykitchen.com
www.refectorykitchen.com

Independent family run brunch and lunch restaurant serving fun and imaginative dishes in a relaxed and friendly atmosphere.

RISE

15 Miller Arcade
Preston
PR1 2QY

44 Fossgate
York
YO1 9TF
www.risebrunch.co.uk
@risebrunch

Independent brunch venue serving stunning coffee and fabulous brunch dishes through the day. A nod to sustainability and an Instagram dream with a chilled and aesthetically pleasing vibe inside and out!

STIR

253 Chesterton Road
Cambridge
CB4 1BG

Unit 1
10 School Hill
Histon
Cambridge
CB24 9JE

Stir Bakery
255 Chesterton Road
Cambridge
CB4 1BG
stircafecambridge@gmail.com
stirbakerycambridge@gmail.com
stirhiston@gmail.com
www.stircambridge.co.uk
@stircambridge @stirbakerycambridge

Independent award-winning café in Cambridge and the village of Histon with a food truck at Chesterton Mill. Proudly serving artisan coffee and delicious brunch as well as cakes, handcrafted pastries and freshly baked bread from their very own bakery. Family friendly and dog friendly.

SUNSET SURF CAFÉ

10 Gwithian Towans
Hayle
TR27 5BT
01736 752575
info@sunset-surf.com
www.sunset-surf.com
@sunset_surf_cafe

Family owned and run business, serving home-cooked, locally sourced food, Cornish coffees and drinks that go down perfectly out on the decking in the sunshine. We pride ourselves on the quality of our food, and on our efficient team and their service – and, of course, our absolutely stunning view.

TAMPER

169 Arundel Street
Sellers Wheel
Sheffield
S1 2NU
0114 275970
www.tampercoffee.co.uk
@tampercoffeesw

Sample a little bit of relaxed Kiwi café culture at Sellers Wheel, a white-washed 19th century former silversmiths in the heart of Sheffield's cultural industries quarter.

THE TERRACE BISTRO

48 London Road
Stockton Heath
Warrington
Cheshire
WA4 6SG
01925738902
info@terracebistro.co.uk
@1terracebistro

The Terrace Bistro offers guests a spacious and contemporary setting to relish in exceptional food and drink in the company of loved ones.

WHERE THE PANCAKES ARE

Arch 35a
85a Southwark Bridge Road
London
SE1 0NQ
020 3838 8810

7-9 Charlotte Street
Fitzrovia
London
W1T 1RG
020 3838 8820
www.wherethepancakesare.com
@wherethepancakesare

We've been bringing people together around pancakes since 2015. Founder Patricia has made it her mission to create pioneering and widely loved pancake restaurants in the heart of London, using fresh quality ingredients to create fluffy American style pancakes beyond your imagination.